the

woman's

hands-on

home

repair

guide

the
woman's
hands-on
home
repair
guide

A STOREY PUBLISHING BOOK

yn

errick

STOREY

To my parents, Carolyn and Graham

*The mission of Storey Publishing is to serve our
customers by publishing practical information that encourages
personal independence in harmony with the environment.*

Edited by Lisa Rathke and Gwen W. Steege
Cover and text design by Mark Tomasi
Cover photograph by Kevin Kennefick
Text production by Eugenie S. Delaney
Line drawings by Alison Kolesar, except pages 174–181 by
Brigita Fuhrmann
Indexed by Nan Badgett
Credit: For assistance related to cover and interior photos,
Aubuchon Hardware, Williamstown, MA, and Security Supply
Corporation, North Adams, MA.

The information in this book is true and complete to the best of
our knowledge. All recommendations are made without guarantee on the part of the author or Storey Publishing. The author and
publisher disclaim any liability in connection with the use of this
information. For additional information please contact Storey
Books, 210 MASS MoCA Way, North Adams, MA 01247.

Storey books are available for special premium and promotional
uses and for customized editions. For further information, please
call the Custom Publishing Department at 1-800-793-9396.

Printed in the United States by R.R. Donnelley & Sons

10 9

Library of Congress Cataloging-in-Publication Data

Herrick, Lyn
    The woman's hands-on home repair guide / by Lyn Herrick
        p.   cm.
    Includes index.
    ISBN 0-88266-973-7 (pbk. : alk. paper)
    1. Dwellings — Maintenance and repair — Amateurs'
    manuals. I. Title.
TH4817.3H474   1997
643'.7—dc21   97-9549
                                                CIP

Contents

Acknowledgments

Research for this book was conducted over the last twenty-five years. It has involved classes, books read, and most importantly, stumbling on my own through many of the projects discussed in the ensuing pages. Several friends have provided me with the necessary training ground in this regard. I appreciate their confidence in me when I tackled projects for the first time in their homes.

I owe a special debt of thanks to my editors at Storey Communications, Gwen Steege and Lisa Rathke. They were both fun to work with and they suggested many changes and additions that greatly strengthened this book. I am deeply grateful to my publisher for believing that this work had merit and for doing so much to bring the book to its current form.

I am also grateful to my husband, Rick. He is the writer in the family and without his encouragement and editorial assistance, I doubt this book would have been written.

My most heartfelt thanks are reserved for two people — my parents, Carolyn and Graham Dripps. I want to thank my mother for a lifetime of love and support. She has always encouraged me to do "my thing" and never complained when I put wrenches on my Christmas list rather than a dress. When I asked her one year for a bulldozer, she did rebel; but that had much more to do with the expense of the gift than its nature. Finally, I want to thank my father, who was my first teacher and most constructive critic. I remember following him around as a little girl, watching with fascination as he fixed an old appliance or a broken window. He never "shooed" me away or suggested that I go find a friend to play with. It is with great love and appreciation that I dedicate this book to them.

Lyn Herrick
Winter 1997

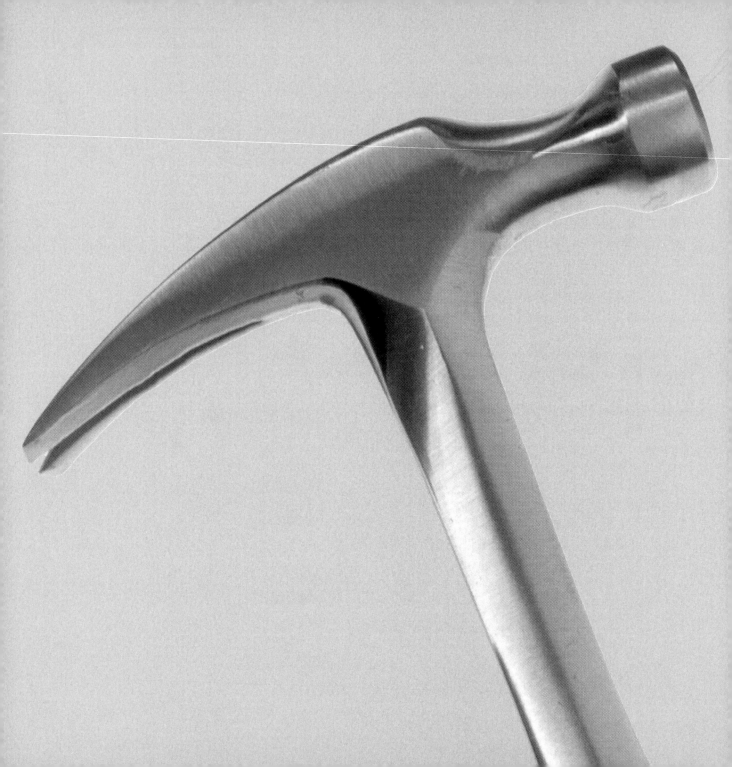

Introduction

Taking Charge

AT A GLANCE

- helpful hints
- basic fix-it rules

and more

Taking Charge of Your Repairs

There is nothing worse than waiting for *somebody else* to fix *your* problem. *The Woman's Hands-On Home Repair Guide* is a how-to book for fixing most of the little, and not so little, things that go wrong in a house or apartment. With the necessary information and the seed of self-confidence, you'll find that you can undertake and complete most repair projects on your own. Even if you are unable to repair the broken object, you will have enough understanding of the problem to talk intelligently to a service person. You'll no longer be afraid of being taken advantage of or appearing ignorant.

Often people assume that they are incapable of solving a problem. However, once they see a friend do it, they become more interested in doing it themselves. Thus, once you become inspired to help yourself, there is no limit to the inspiration you can give to others. Go into each project knowing that you can do it, laugh at your mistakes, and you will be surprised how many friends you make in your journey toward self-sufficiency.

There are many funny stories in connection with my fixing projects. Some were not funny at the time, but in retrospect can be laughed at. After you have undertaken a few of the tasks in this book, you may have some amusing incidents to relate. More importantly, I hope that you will have gained the confidence to continue to fix and to learn more about how things work and why they don't work.

How To Use This Book

Each section opens with a trouble-shooting chart that lists the problems, probable causes, remedies, and page numbers to turn to so that you can find the information you need quickly. Look for the list of tools you'll need to assemble before starting to work. Step-by-step instructions for repairs are accompanied by invaluable tips for making repairs easily and safely, as well as suggestions for making things last longer and operate with greater efficiency. Tips are contained in three boxes throughout the book, labeled Safety Tip, Energy Saver, and Making It Last. Quick repair advice is provided in the circles marked with a wrench. The appendix lists the basic tools you'll need for most projects and how to use them.

The illustrations are designed for easy understanding. Please note that your fixtures or appliances may not be identical to those illustrated. However, in most cases the principles will be the same and you will be able to apply what you see in the drawings to your own situation.

Before undertaking any project, it's a good idea to get thoroughly familiar with the book. You'll find suggestions for locating various valves and switches *before* you have an emergency. It's especially important to learn where and how to turn off electricity and water. With a little bit of prior knowledge, you will be able to handle just about any situation efficiently and confidently.

Helpful Hints

Before you set out on your fixing projects, here are some tips on what tools and parts to buy, where to buy them, and how to maintain them.

• This book refers to hardware stores, building supply stores, electrical supply stores, and plumbing supply stores. In different parts of the country, different types of stores carry the necessary parts and pieces for the projects you'll need to address. Some large building supply stores will have most of the repair and replacement parts that you need. It is very helpful and convenient to find a hardware store that carries "just about anything." The advantage to these types of stores is that the employees

BARGAINS AREN'T ALWAYS BETTER

I am usually a price-conscious shopper, and prices for repair supplies can differ significantly among different stores. In some fixing situations, however, it's more important to deal with a knowledgeable salesperson than it is to get the lowest price. If you are repairing a leaking faucet, it is probably cheaper to purchase the replacement parts at a large discount store rather than at a plumbing supply store. The trouble is that you may get into the middle of the project and not know how to finish it. The salesperson at the plumbing supply store will most likely be able to guide you to completion. I wouldn't count on receiving similar advice at the large discount store. So shop around for an appropriate store like you would for a doctor. It will pay in the long run.

usually know something about everything and they can be very helpful if you are having problems.

- Keep all service manuals and receipts for your household purchases and automobile needs. Maintain these manuals and receipts in a file for the life of the part, appliance, etc. These manuals and receipts are invaluable for determining parts numbers, dates of purchase, extent of warranty, and so on.

- In order to accomplish even the simplest task around the house, you must have a supply of basic tools. Assemble yourself a small but useful tool chest. Here is a list of basic tools to include. For a discussion of how to use these tools, see pages 176–183.

Straight-slot screw-driver	Portable electric drill	Crosscut saw
Steel tape measure	Pipe wrench	Pliers
Phillips screwdriver	Utility knife	Hacksaw
Long-nose pliers	Pipe cutter	Hammer
Adjustable wrench	Putty knife	WD40
	Vise grip	

Basic Fix-It Rules

Rule #1. Always turn **off** the power or the water or both when working on any of these projects. (See pages 8–9 and 40–43.) With electricity, this rule is crucial to your safety. With plumbing, it may help avert a flood.

Rule #2. Take one step at a time and read the directions before you start your project. Make sure you note what is connected to what as you disassemble something. Mark all wires and make diagrams and notes if you are faced with putting something back together. Even though a project looks easy, read the directions if you have them. This will save time and aggravation.

Rule #3. "Right is tight and left is loose." Remember that to tighten screws and nuts you turn them clockwise or to the right. To loosen them, turn them counterclockwise or to the left. In a few situations you will turn them the opposite direction. Bike pedals and an occasional plumbing part will be threaded backwards. If you cannot get a screw or nut tightened by turning it to the right, try the other direction. Sometimes the threads on the screw or nut are stripped or damaged and will not tighten in either direction. In this case, replace the defective fastener.

Rule #4. Do not start a project with a limited amount of time available. You need to be able to take your time to understand what is happening. Nothing ever takes as short a time as you would like. You do not want to rush anything. Rushing only causes problems.

Rule #5. Dress properly for these projects. Plan to get dirty or wet while undertaking these fix-it repairs. You may not get dirty or wet, but it is wise to be prepared for it.

Rule #6. Be aware of plumbing and electrical code law. In both cases, these laws are written by local governments. The general rule is that an individual may undertake repairs that restore an electrical or plumbing component of their house to its original condition. For changes or additions to your plumbing or electrical systems, a permit may be required. Consult your local building inspector.

SEAL OF APPROVAL

Make sure when purchasing electrical appliances and supplies that the item has the Underwriters' Laboratories (UL) seal of approval attached to it. Underwriters' Laboratories is an independent organization that tests all consumer electrical products to ensure their safety and effectiveness.

Chapter One

Plumbing

Anatomy of a Home Water System

Water from a public utility or your well enters your home through a large supply pipe. If you purchase your water from a public utility, it passes through a meter on its way into the house. The supply pipe then splits into two lines, one of which goes to the water heater.

Proceeding from the water heater is a hot-water line that runs parallel with the cold-water line to every plumbing fixture in your home. These supply lines move water through the house at a constant pressure, usually between 50 and 60 pounds per square inch.

Your plumbing system also includes a waste system consisting of a series of pipes that carry waste from your house to a city sewer or your septic tank. These pipes use gravity, rather than water pressure, to do their work. Another set of pipes vents gases and odors to the outside of the house. In addition to these vent pipes, drain traps located under your sinks prevent gases from going back into your home. These U-shaped pipes allow running water to flow down through them, but when the faucet is turned off, the water that lies "trapped" at the bottom of the pipe acts as a barrier to prevent gases from re-entering your home.

How to Turn Off the Water

If you have a leak or are repairing a plumbing fixture, you must turn off the water going into that fixture before beginning your work.

<u>Tool to Have on Hand:</u> large adjustable wrench

Unless you have a very old house or a poorly planned one, you will find water shut-off valves under each of your plumbing fixtures. Bathroom and kitchen sinks have both hot- and cold-water shut-off valves, while toilets have only cold-water valves. In some cases these shut-off valves are in the basement or crawl space under the house.

If the sink, toilet, or shower you are working on does not have a shut-off valve, you will have to turn off all the water in the house at the main shut-off valve. This valve is found near the water meter or close to the wall where the main water line enters the house. If you must use the main shut-off valve, it is important to make sure that the power to your water heater is turned off. To do this, turn off the circuit breaker switch that reg-

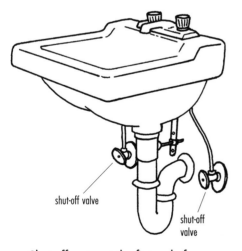

shut-off valve

shut-off valve

Shut off water at the fixture before making repair.

ulates the operation of the water heater (see pages 40–41).

If you get your water from the city or a source other than your own well or spring, there may also be a shut-off valve out in the yard near the street. You will often find this meter in a small hole in the yard, covered by a heavy metal lid. Remove the lid and use a large adjustable wrench to turn the valve. Sometimes a special wrench is required. If this is so, check with your water supplier about obtaining access to this wrench.

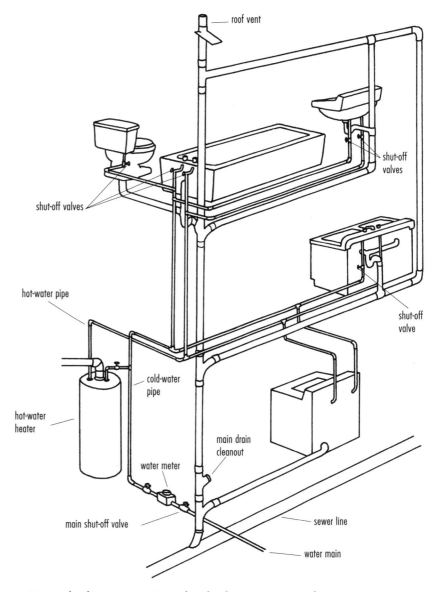

Home plumbing system. Note that the thinner pipes are the incoming hot- and cold-water pipes; the thick pipes are the drains and vents.

Hot Water Problems

Gas

PROBLEM	CAUSE	REMEDY	PAGE
Water too hot	Thermostat set too high	Turn temperature down	11
Water not hot enough	Thermostat set too low	Turn temperature up	11
Water cold	Heater not turning on	Relight pilot light; fill gas tank	13
Water leaking from tank	Worn-out tank	Replace heater	

Electric

PROBLEM	CAUSE	REMEDY	PAGE
Water too hot	Thermostat set too high	Turn temperature down	11
Water not hot enough	Thermostat set too low	Turn temperature up	11
Water cold	Heating element burned out	Replace element	12–13
Uses too much electricity	Heater on all the time	Install timer	11
Water leaking from tank	Worn-out tank	Replace heater	

straight-slot screw and screwdriver

Phillips screw and screwdriver

hex screw and adjustable wrench

Screws and their corresponding tools

Regulating Your Water Heater

One of the most expensive household appliances in terms of purchase price and energy costs is the water heater. You can make many simple and relatively quick adjustments to this appliance to reduce energy costs and repair bills. The most typical water heaters are either gas-fired or electricity-powered. Oil-fired water heaters were common twenty-five years ago but are not usually used today. Determine what kind of heater you have before undertaking any of the projects below.

It is usually not necessary to have your water heater set on the maximum temperature, yet many people keep their water heater far too high. You can save both money and energy without reducing the amount of hot water you need if you set your heater at a lower reading.

<u>Tools to Have on Hand:</u> straight-slot screwdriver, Phillips screwdriver, small adjustable wrench

Gas-fired water heaters. An adjustable thermostat is located where the gas connection joins with the tank. Just turn this thermostat to the desired temperature. Although you may often find this set at 140° to 150°F, you can turn it down to 120° to 130°F and experiment with your needs. If you then find that the water is not hot enough, just turn the thermostat back up.

Electric water heaters. These heaters have two thermostats, each of which regulates a heating element in the tank. These thermostats are located under two removable panels on the side of the water heater — one at the top and the other on the bottom. The panels are held in place with small screws. Disconnect the power supply before removing panels.

Unfasten the screws from the panels and remove the panels. You will see a dial with markings that range from 100° to 150°F. As stated above, the normal temperature setting is 140° to 150°F. Experiment with setting the dial at 120°F. The temperature on our heater is set at that level, and the water is still hot enough for our family of five. If you have a dishwasher that will not operate efficiently at temperatures under 140°F, you may have to keep the thermostat set higher.

The pointer on each dial is what moves, not the dial. Move the pointer from 150° to 120°F on both the top and bottom dials. When you have reset the dials, put the panels back on. That's all there is to it.

Gas hot water heater

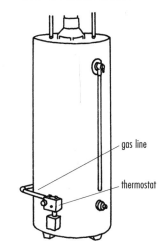

gas line

thermostat

The thermostat for a gas hot water heater is located where the gas line comes into the appliance.

Electric hot water heater

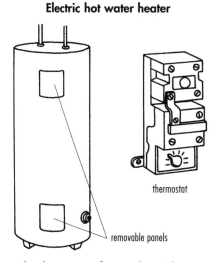

thermostat

removable panels

The thermostats for an electric hot water heater are located behind removable panels.

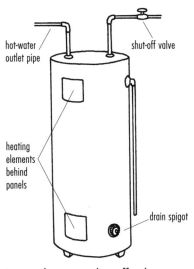

hot-water outlet pipe

shut-off valve

heating elements behind panels

drain spigot

Locate the water shut-off valve before beginning the repair.

Bolt-on heating element

Replacing Elements in Electric Water Heaters

If you have an electric water heater, and your water is only warm when the thermostat is properly set, then you have probably burned out one or both of the heating elements.

<u>Tools to Have on Hand:</u> adjustable wrench, straight-slot or Phillips screwdriver, large hex wrench

There are many different types of elements, so don't try to buy a new one before taking the old one out. Some elements bolt on and some screw in. Depending on the type you have, you will need an adjustable wrench, a Phillips screwdriver, or a straight-slot screwdriver. Screw-in heater elements require a specially designed wrench, an inexpensive tool that can be purchased at an appliance parts store. Replacing a heating element is not too difficult, but you must proceed cautiously to avoid a few potential disasters.

1. Turn off the circuit breaker or remove the fuse that regulates the water heater. Turn off the water that is going into the heater in order to protect against flooding the basement. To do this, find the shut-off valve on the line going into the top of the water heater. Turn this valve clockwise.

2. Drain the water heater. First, open a hot-water faucet somewhere in the house to break the vacuum. Find the spigot at the bottom of the heater and attach a regular garden hose to the spigot. Then run the hose outside of the house. Turn the spigot on. Water heaters hold lots of water, so be patient while it fully drains.

3. Remove the heating elements, which are located in the same panels as the thermostats. There is a top and a bottom element. If you are not sure which element is burned out and you do not have an element tester, it is best to remove both elements and take them to the store for testing.

4. Four bolts or screws hold each element to the side of the tank. Within the area outlined by the bolts or screws are two wires that connect the element to the terminal above. Mark the top wire by taping it. Begin disconnecting the two wires by loosening the screws.

Bolt-on elements. Unfasten each bolt, and the element will slide out toward you.

Screw-in elements. The end you see will look like a large, flat hex nut. Place the special wrench over the end and put a screwdriver through the small holes at the opposite end. Use screwdriver for leverage while turning the element counterclockwise. Once loosened, remove the element by sliding it out.

Screw-in heating element

5. Take the old element to an appliance store to replace it exactly.

6. Insert the new element by reversing the process. Slide the good element into place and refasten the two wires to the appropriate screws, making sure that the one you marked with tape is placed on top. Then tighten each of the four bolts.

7. Replace the two panels, remove the garden hose, and turn the bottom spigot off.

8. Run water back into the heater by turning on the line at the top of the heater.

9. When the water heater is full, turn the circuit breaker back on.

MAKING IT LAST

When to Turn the Circuit Breaker Back On

When it's time to refill the water heater, turn on a hot-water tap where you can observe it. When the water begins to run in a steady flow from this tap, you will know that your water heater is full. Only when the heater is completely full of water can you turn on the circuit breaker switch controlling the water heater. Some heating elements will burn out without water passing through them, so be careful not to turn the circuit breaker on too quickly or leave the water heater on when the water to the tank is turned off.

ENERGY SAVER

Lowering Your Hot-Water Bill

- Make sure your water heater is properly insulated. If you believe you need more insulation, consult a plumber because there are some safety considerations involved in adding additional insulation.
- Lower the temperature on your water heater to 120°F.
- Repair leaky hot-water faucets promptly.
- Do as much household cleaning as possible using cold water.

Problems with Gas Water Heaters

When a gas water heater is not heating the water properly, the problem is probably with the gas supply. There should be a pilot light that remains lit continuously, so that when the thermostat triggers the heater to go on, the pilot will light the burner. If the pilot light is not burning and you are using propane instead of natural gas, the main gas tank may be empty. Check the fuel gauge on the tank. If it is not empty, try relighting the pilot light. The instructions for lighting the pilot will be found on a plate on the water heater.

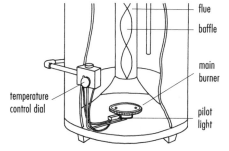

Cutaway of gas hot water heater, showing pilot light

Leaky Kitchen Sink Fixtures

PROBLEM	CAUSE	REMEDY	PAGE
Leaky spigot	Worn-out washers and springs	Replace washer and springs	15
	Worn-out cartridge	Replace cartridge	16
	Worn-out valve assembly	Replace damaged parts	16–17
Leaky faucet base	Worn-out O-rings	Replace O-rings	17
Leaky sprayer	Connections loose	Tighten connections	17
	Washer worn	Replace washer	17
	Spray nozzle worn	Replace spray nozzle	17
Leaky water supply pipe	Damaged pipe	Replace pipe	17

Disassembling Parts
Lay out the parts in order as you disassemble the faucet so that you replace them properly.

Most kitchen sinks contain noncompression faucets. A noncompression faucet has a single lever that regulates the flow of both hot and cold water with a rotating ball, cartridge, or valve mechanism. A drip at the spout generally means that one of the working parts needs replacing. The good news is that you can purchase prepackaged repair kits that contain all the necessary replacement parts as well as directions for completing the repair task.

Your first step, therefore, is to determine the exact make and model of your faucet and purchase the appropriate repair kit at your local hardware or plumbing supply store.

<u>Tool to Have on Hand:</u> adjustable wrench

Rotating Ball Faucets

A rotating ball faucet has a ball with three openings, one for hot water, one for cold water, and a third for the spout. Moving the faucet handle controls both the rate of flow and the temperature of the water.

This style of faucet often works for years without problems. Over time, leaks may develop at the spigot or the base of the faucet.

<u>Tools to Have on Hand:</u> Allen wrench (if not in repair kit), pipe wrench, long-nosed pliers, kitchen knife

Repairing leaky spigot. If your faucet drips at the spigot, it is likely that the springs and small rubber seals need replacing.

1. Turn off the water under the sink before starting the project.

2. Remove the set screw at the base of the handle with either an Allen wrench or the small wrench that comes in the repair kit. Now you will be able to pull off the handle.

3. Wrap the serrated sleeve of the cap with tape to protect its finish and unscrew it with a plumber's wrench. This will expose the ball-and-cam assembly, which you can pull out with your fingers.

4. Look into what is left of the faucet and you will see two holes. In each hole there is a spring and a small black rubber washer. Remove them with your fingers or with long-nose pliers. Replace them with new, identical parts from the repair kit. The springs go into the holes first, followed by the washers, whose cupped sides fit over the springs.

5. Before putting the faucet back together, check the ball for chips or scratches. If there are some, replace the ball too.

6. To reassemble the faucet, look for a slot on the ball. It must line up with a metal pin within the faucet body. The cam assembly should line up with the same slot.

Repairing leak at faucet base. If the leak occurs at the base of the faucet, you will need to replace the O-rings.

1. Turn off the water under the sink.

2. Disassemble the faucet as outlined above.

3. Remove the spout by pulling it up and working it from side-to-side. This will expose one or more O-rings.

4. With a knife or screwdriver, slip the old O-rings from the faucet. If O-rings are not included in the repair kit, purchase exact replacements at the hardware store.

5. Insert the new O-rings and reassemble the faucet.

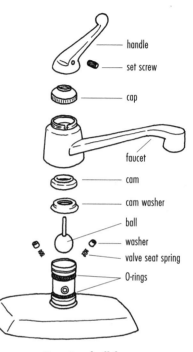

Rotating ball faucet

handle
set screw
cap
faucet
cam
cam washer
ball
washer
valve seat spring
O-rings

Installing O-Rings
It often helps when inserting the new O-rings to grease the faucet base with a silicone-based grease.

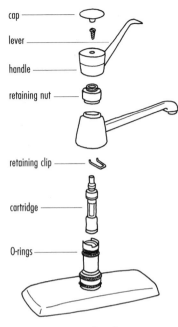

cap

lever

handle

retaining nut

retaining clip

cartridge

O-rings

Cartridge faucet

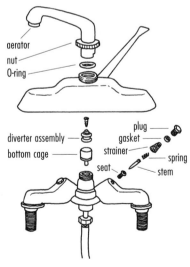

aerator

nut

O-ring

diverter assembly

bottom cage

seat

plug

gasket

strainer

spring

stem

Valve faucet

Cartridge Faucets

A cartridge faucet substitutes a cartridge for the rotating ball. The cartridge has similar openings for hot and cold water. Manipulating the handle controls the flow of water and the water temperature. This type of faucet is even simpler to work with. For leaks at the base of the faucet, replace the O-rings as discussed on the previous page.

<u>Tools to Have on Hand:</u> straight-slot screwdriver, kitchen knife

Repairing leaky spigot. A leaky faucet requires that you replace the cartridge stem, as follows:

1. Shut off the water underneath the sink.
2. Take off the decorative cap, remove the screw, and pry the handle off with a screwdriver.
3. Locate the retaining clip where the handle meets the base of the faucet.
4. Pry the retaining clip out with a screwdriver.
5. Pull the cartridge out with your fingers.
6. Install the new cartridge, making sure that the arrow or identifying mark on the cartridge is pointing up.
7. Insert retaining clip and reassemble faucet.

Valve Faucets

Valve faucets are most like the two-handled compression faucets found in your bathroom except that they have no washers and a single lever controls the hot and cold water. Moving the lever opens up valves on either the hot- or cold-water side, which allows water to enter the spout.

<u>Tools to Have on Hand:</u> pipe wrench or large adjustable wrench, small adjustable wrench, hexagonal seat wrench

Repairing leaky spigot. When valve faucets leak, disassemble the fixture to determine faulty parts, as follows:

1. Turn off the water under the sink.
2. Tape the nut at the spout's base to protect the spigot from getting scratched.
3. Loosen the nut with a pipe wrench or large adjustable wrench and then lift the spout straight up and off.

4. Continue disassembling the faucet by lifting off the body cover. This will expose two hexagonal plugs — one on each side of the faucet. With a small wrench remove each plug.

5. Now you will see a gasket, strainer, spring, stem, and seat. Remove the gasket, strainer, spring, and stem with your fingers. Use a hexagonal seat wrench and fit the tapered end of the wrench onto the valve seat to dislodge it.

6. Examine all parts for wear or damage and replace worn parts with exact replicas.

7. Reassemble the faucet in reverse order.

Repairing leak around the base. If your faucet leaks around the base, replace the O-rings as described for rotating ball faucets (page 15).

Leaky Sprayer

Leaks may develop around the hose or spray nozzle of your kitchen sprayer. First tighten these connections and see if that solves the problem. If the leak remains, turn off the water at the faucet, take apart the sprayer by unscrewing the spray nozzle from the hose, and replace the washers. The problem may also be caused by a faulty diverter, which can also be replaced. If the sprayer continues to leak, purchase a replacement nozzle at the hardware store and screw it on.

Leaky Water Supply Pipe

If a water pipe under your kitchen sink starts to leak, you will need to replace the pipe.

<u>Tool to Have on Hand:</u> adjustable wrench

1. Turn off the water at the shut-off valves under the sink.

2. With an adjustable wrench, disconnect the pipe at both ends.

3. Take the damaged pipe with you to the hardware store and purchase a replacement pipe.

4. Connect the new pipe to the fixture and the outlet valves. Some pipes come with plastic wing nuts that you hand-tighten, others come with metal nuts that you tighten with an adjustable wrench.

5. Once installed, turn on the water to check for leaks. If you find some, tighten further. Your water pipe should no longer leak.

Sink sprayer

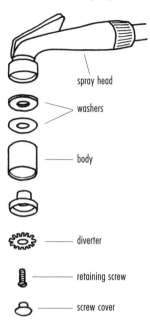

spray head

washers

body

diverter

retaining screw

screw cover

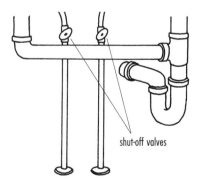

shut-off valves

The water supply pipes are the narrower pipes behind the thick drain pipes. Note the two shut-off valves.

Leaky Bathroom Sink Faucet

CAUSE	REMEDY	PAGE
Worn out washer	Replace washer	18–19
Worn out valve seat	Replace or regrind valve seat	19
Worn out O-ring	Replace O-ring	15

Organizing Parts
As you remove faucet parts, lay them out in order of disassembly so that you reassemble them properly.

The most common bathroom faucet is a compression faucet, which has separate handles for hot and cold water. When the handle is turned off, a washer on the bottom of the stem is forced against a valve seat, blocking the water flow.

If the faucet drips, you probably need a new washer. Another possibility is a damaged valve seat, which will need to be reground or replaced. Finally, if the leak is coming from the base of the handle, the O-rings are the problem (see page 15 for repair advice). If your bathroom sink has a cartridge faucet, see page 16 for repairing leaky cartridge faucets.

<u>Tools to Have on Hand:</u> straight-slot or Phillips screwdriver, adjustable wrench, seat wrench (as needed), seat grinding tool (as needed)

Replacing the Washer

1. Feel the temperature of the leaking water to determine which faucet — hot or cold — is the problem.

2. Turn off the water going to the leaky faucet at the shut-off valve under the sink, against the wall.

3. Pop or pry off the appropriate "H" or "C" cap on top of the handle, unscrew the handle, and pry the handle up and off.

4. Wrap a rag or tape around the packing nut to protect the fixture from being scratched. Unscrew the packing nut with an adjustable wrench by turning it counterclockwise.

5. Remove the stem by pulling it up.

6. With the stem removed, examine the washer that sits at the end of the stem. If the washer is damaged or worn, water is able to leak through the damaged area and drip into the sink.

Pry off the screw cap, then unfasten the screw to remove the handle.

7. With a screwdriver, remove the screw that holds the washer in place and take out the washer.

8. Replace the old washer with a new one exactly like it. You will also want to replace the screw if it is badly worn or corroded.

9. Screw the stem and packing nut back into the sink, and reassemble the handle.

10. Turn on the water valve under the sink and check to see if the problem is fixed.

Replacing the Valve Seat

If the drip remains, the valve seat is probably the problem. The valve seat is the little brass ring upon which the washer sits. When a seat is nicked or cracked, it is not able to hold the water back. You will need to purchase a seat wrench for this project (see drawing below, right). This wrench is handy to have and is not expensive.

1. Turn off the water at the shut-off valve.

2. Remove handle and stem of faucet as described in immediately preceding section.

3. Fit the seat wrench into the square or hexagonal opening in the middle of the valve seat and unscrew it.

4. Lift the valve seat out of the faucet and examine it. If it is worn, notched, or cracked, it will need to be replaced with an exact duplicate.

5. Place the new seat on the end of the wrench and screw it back into place. Reassemble the stem and handle.

Grinding the Valve Seat

Some faucets have nonremovable valve seats. In this case you will need to purchase a seat grinding tool, an inexpensive device (see drawing at right).

1. Insert the seat grinding tool into the faucet hole so that the tool's cutting edge sits on the valve seat.

2. Turn the handle back and forth several times while applying light downward pressure. You want to smooth the seat, not grind it down.

3. Wash the loose pieces of metal away and reassemble the faucet. The drip should now be fixed.

Compression faucet

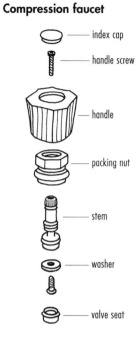

index cap

handle screw

handle

packing nut

stem

washer

valve seat

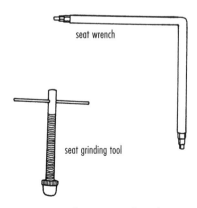

seat wrench

seat grinding tool

You can purchase a small tool to grind the valve seat, if necessary.

Leaky Bathtub or Shower Faucet

PROBLEM	CAUSE	REMEDY	PAGE
Faucet leaks or drips	Worn-out washer	Replace washer	20
	Worn-out valve seat	Replace valve seat	21
Shower head leaks	Worn-out washer	Replace washer	21

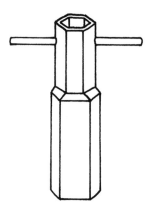

You can purchase a special wrench for removing the shower faucet.

Leaky or Drippy Bathtub Faucet

If the bathtub faucet leaks or drips, you fix it the same way that you fix bathroom sink leaks, with two exceptions.

First, the water shut-off valves for the shower are often located in hard-to-reach places. Therefore, the best approach is to turn off all the water in the house. Allow the water to drain out before beginning to work.

Second, most stems on bathtub faucets are recessed into the wall or the shell of the tub. To remove the stem, you will need to purchase a special stem wrench from the hardware or plumbing supply store (see drawing at left). This is not an expensive wrench and is certainly cheaper than calling a plumber. These wrenches come in various sizes. Tell the salesperson what kind of fixture you have and he/she should be able to get you the right size wrench.

Tools to Have on Hand: straight-slot or Phillips screwdriver, stem wrench, seat wrench (as needed)

Replacing the Washer. The first thing to look for in a leaky faucet is a worn-out washer.

1. Turn off the main water valve.

2. Take off the faucet handle by prying off the decorative cap, unscrewing the little screw, and then prying off the handle with a screwdriver.

3. Once the handle is removed, insert the wrench onto the stem. Stick a screwdriver through the hole at the end of the wrench. Using the screwdriver as a handle, unscrew the stem and remove it.

4. Look at the washer and replace it if it is worn or nicked.

5. Reassemble the stem and the handle.

Replacing the Valve Seat.
If the leak continues, the valve seat, the brass ring under the washer, may be damaged or worn.

1. Turn off main water valve.

2. Remove faucet handle and stem as described on page 20.

3. Fit the seat wrench into the square or hexagonal opening in the middle of the valve seat and unscrew it.

4. Lift the valve seat out of the faucet and examine it. If it is worn, notched, or cracked, replace with an exact duplicate.

5. Place the new valve seat on the end of the wrench and screw it into place.

6. Reassemble the stem and handle.

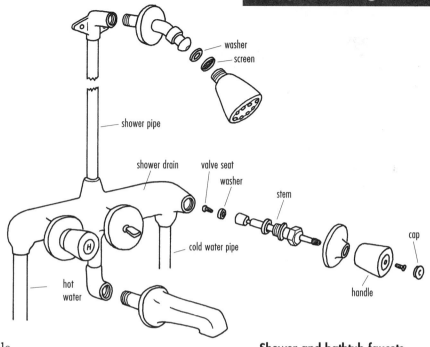

Shower and bathtub faucets

Leaky Shower Head
<u>Tools to Have on Hand</u>: straight-slot or Phillips screwdriver

If the shower head drips when turned off, simply unscrew the head and replace the washer that fits inside the opening.

Repairing Shower Door
When your shower door goes off track, it is easy to fix.
<u>Tools to Have on Hand</u>: straight-slot screwdriver, long-nose pliers

Gravity holds these doors in place. Just lift up the door and put the wheels back in the track. Check the condition of your wheels. If they are worn, then they are probably not working too well. This forces you to pull harder when trying to move the door, which gets them off the track. Purchase a new set of wheels at a hardware store and replace the old ones. Check the condition of the track, too. Remove any kinks by bending them out with long-nose pliers.

Solving Water Flow Problems

PROBLEM	CAUSE	REMEDY	PAGE
Water trickles from faucet	Clogged aerator	Clean aerator	22
	Main shut-off valve left partially turned off	Turn shut-off valve all the way on	22
	Inadequate pressure	Call public utility or a plumber	22
	Supply pipes clogged	Call plumber	22
Water trickles from shower	Shower head clogged with sediment	Clean shower head	23

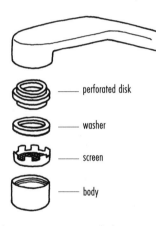

— perforated disk

— washer

— screen

— body

The aerator can easily be removed for cleaning.

Trickling Faucet

If one of your faucets only trickles when turned on, the problem may be a clogged aerator.

1. Unscrew the aerator at the end of the spigot and turn on the water. If it flows rapidly, your problem is in the aerator.

2. Clean out the screen in the aerator and put it back on the spigot.

3. Turn on the water and test the flow.

If the trickling occurs in other faucets in the house at the same time, you have a more complicated problem to solve. Check the main shut-off valve. If you are lucky, it was left partially turned off and you can solve the problem by turning it all the way on.

Most likely, however, the problem resides elsewhere. You may be receiving inadequate pressure either from the water company's main or from your private well. If you receive your water from a public utility, check to see if your neighbors are experiencing a similar problem. Also look for soggy areas on your lawn, which indicate a leak in the pipe between your house and the public utility's main. In either case, call the public utility and have them investigate the problem. If you have a private well, consult a plumber.

Another possibility is that the supply pipes inside your home are clogged. Again, this is a job best left to a professional.

Trickling or Weak Shower

If the water pressure from your shower is weak or uneven, most likely the shower head needs to be cleaned.

<u>Tools to Have on Hand:</u> toothpick or ice pick, adjustable wrench

Sediment often gathers in the narrow grooves behind the water deflector cap. Remove the sediment with a toothpick or an ice pick. You can also take off the shower head and soak it overnight in vinegar, which will dissolve the sediment. Use a pipe wrench to unscrew the nut that fastens the shower head to the shower arm (see drawing on page 21). To protect the chrome finish on the shower head, wrap the nut with adhesive tape before using a wrench to take off the head.

Installing a Hand-Held Shower

Hand-held showers are an inexpensive luxury that can be purchased at any plumbing supply store. They are also simple to install.

<u>Tool to Have on Hand:</u> pipe wrench

1. Begin by turning off the water to the shower from the main shut-off valve into your home.

2. Some models merely replace the shower head. Unscrew the old shower head with a pipe wrench at the base of the shower arm and replace it with your new hand-held shower hose and you are done.

3. Other, more fancy, models come with an assembly that allows you to keep the old shower head. Again, take off the old shower head at the base of the shower arm.

4. Attach the new assembly that provides outlets for the old shower head and the hand-held shower hose.

5. Finally, screw in the old shower head and the new hand-held shower hose and the job is done.

Toilet That Runs Constantly

CAUSE	REMEDY	PAGE
Water level too high in tank	Adjust water level	24
	Replace shut-off valve	25

Toilets that continually run in between flushes waste a lot of water. You can tell if a toilet is using water in between flushes by the sound in the tank and the ripples of running water in the toilet bowl. Lift the tank to see what is going on. You will notice an overflow tube and water in the tank. If the water level is too high, the water spills into the tube, creating the problem.

Adjusting the Water Level

You will need to adjust the water level to just below the opening at the top of the overflow tube. The water level is regulated by the large ball that floats in the tank. A brass arm connects the ball to a shut-off valve. As the water in the tank rises and the ball floats upward, it creates downward pressure on the shut-off valve, which eventually closes. To make the shut-off valve close more quickly, you need to increase the downward angle of the brass arm.

1. Screw the ball in a little on the connecting arm so that the distance between the shut-off valve and ball is reduced.

2. If the ball is completely screwed in, gently bend the connecting arm so that the ball is lower in the water.

3. Flush the toilet and see how high the water rises in the tank. If it still rises above the mouth of the tube, gently bend the float arm further so that the ball sits even lower in the water.

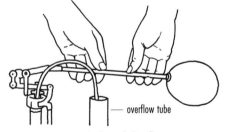

overflow tube

Step 2: Gently bend the float arm.

Replacing the Shut-Off Valve

Occasionally this problem results from a defective shut-off valve. If the water won't shut off as you pull up on the ball, replace the old valve mechanism with a new self-contained plastic mechanism that can be purchased at any hardware or plumbing supply store.

<u>Tools to Have on Hand:</u> two adjustable wrenches

1. Flush the toilet and close the water intake valve under the toilet tank.

2. Place a pan or bucket under the tank to catch any water that remains in the tank. Place an adjustable wrench onto the nut of the old mechanism and use another wrench to loosen the nut under the tank that holds the old mechanism in place. Now remove the old mechanism.

3. To install the new plastic mechanism, follow the instructions on the package.

This new plastic mechanism regulates the water level according to the pressure in the tank. To increase the water level, turn the knob at the base of the regulator mechanism clockwise. To decrease the water level, turn the knob counterclockwise. Start with one turn at a time and check the water level.

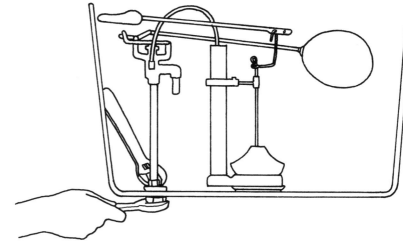

Step 2: Remove the old shut-off mechanism and ball system at the base of the tank.

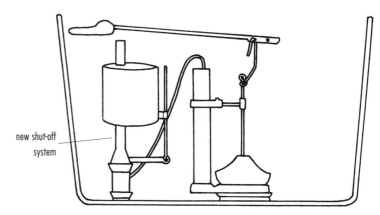

new shut-off system

Step 3: Replace the shut-off valve with a new plastic system, following the instructions on the package.

Toilets That Won't Flush

CAUSE	REMEDY	PAGE
Not enough water in tank	Adjust water level	26
	Fix plug in bottom of tank	26

When the tank does not fill up with enough water, the toilet does not flush completely. The solution is to raise the water level in the tank.

<u>Tool to Have on Hand:</u> straight-slot screwdriver (as needed)

To adjust the water level, follow these steps. For toilets with a plastic mechanism, turn the knob at the base of the regulator clockwise. For older toilets with a floating ball, lengthen the distance between the ball and the shut-off valve by unscrewing the ball on the connecting arm a little. If the ball is unscrewed as far as it will go, gently bend the connecting arm up.

Flush the toilet to check the new level of the water. You want the water to sit about ¾-inch from the top of the tube.

If the toilet does not flush at all, the likely cause is that the water in the tank is leaking out as rapidly as it enters. At the bottom of the tank a rubber ball sits on an opening. When the toilet is flushed, the ball is forced up by the toilet handle allowing water to flow out of the tank. When the tank empties, the ball falls back on the hole and forms a seal against the opening as the tank again fills with water. As the ball becomes worn, water leaks out of the tank. The solution is to replace the ball so that you will once again have a proper seal.

1. Shut off the water to the toilet by closing off the valve underneath the toilet tank. You don't want water rushing into the tank while you work.

2. Remove the old ball. The ball may be attached by a collar slipped over the overflow tube, a hook connected to two hooks on the side of the overflow tube, or in older models, a chain linked to a lever, which is connected to the flush handle. In some toilets the ball is screwed into a metal piece connected to the lever. Simply raise the ball up and unscrew it.

shut-off valve

Step 1: Before working on the toilet, shut off the water at the base of the intake pipe.

3. Take the old ball to the hardware store to replace it. If you have a ball with a chain, it is unlikely that you will be able to replace it exactly. Instead you can purchase a new flapper mechanism. The flapper slips onto the overflow tube and comes with a chain that connects to the flush handle. You will need to adjust the chain so that the flapper rises and then sits snugly over the hole in the tank (see drawing at right).

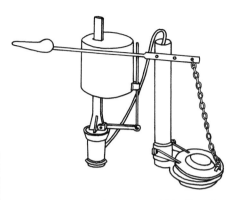

You may replace your old ball and chain mechanism with this flapper and chain version.

ENERGY SAVER

A More Efficient Toilet

The average commode uses 5 gallons of water per flush, although only 3 gallons are actually needed. New, highly efficient toilets use only 1.6 gallons per flush. You can reduce the amount of water in your commode by inserting a simple water displacement device. Two possibilities include a plastic bottle filled with water or a brick covered with plastic (you do not want the brick to decompose in the water). These devices will displace about one or two quarts of water and reduce the flush accordingly. Be aware that they may also affect the flushing action.

MAKING IT LAST

Repairing Leaks Around the Sink and Tub

Water can leak into the cracks around the rim of your bathroom sink or between the sink countertop and the wall. Similar problems also occur along the edge of your bathroom tub. Leaking water creates mildew and musty odors, and it may do structural damage. Apply silicone caulk to seal these cracks.

Unclogging the Kitchen Sink Drain

PROBLEM	CAUSE	REMEDY	PAGE
Clogged drain	Garbage disposal full	Turn on disposal	
	Drain blocked with gunk	Use plunger, hose, or sink auger	28
	Drain trap blocked	Clean out drain trap	29
	Roots grown into water drain line outside of house	Call repair service	

A clogged drain is frustrating and always seems to happen when the kitchen sink is full of dirty dishes. But don't despair — you can solve the problem easily without calling a plumber.

<u>Tools to Have on Hand:</u> plunger, garden hose (as needed), adjustable wrench (as needed), pipe wrench (as needed), wire coat hanger (as needed), sink auger (as needed)

Plunging the Drain

1. Run a little water into the sink.
2. Place a plunger on top of the drain.
3. Push down hard and pull up on the plunger.
4. Repeat several times. That should loosen the blockage and the water should now drain smoothly.

Flushing the Drain with a Hose

If the plunger method doesn't work, try using a garden hose.

1. Lead your garden hose from an outside spigot to the problem drain.
2. Insert the hose into the drain and stuff a towel around and inside the drain hole to make a tight seal.
3. Have a friend turn on the water at the outside faucet while you hold the hose in the drain. That may flush out the debris and clear the pipes.

Cleaning the Drain Trap

If that fails, you may need to clean the drain trap, the U-shaped pipe under the sink. The drain trap is filled with water at all times to prevent sewer gas, pests such as rats, and other unpleasant contaminants from entering your house through the pipe. In other words, drain traps perform an important function in your home. Unfortunately, they also become clogged.

1. Place a small bucket or shallow pan under the trap to catch any water that remains in the sink drain.

2. Some traps have a plug at the bottom that can easily be removed for cleaning. Unfasten the plug using an adjustable wrench. If your pipe does not have a clean-out plug, remove the entire trap. Use a plumber's wrench to unfasten the two nuts that connect the trap to the drain pipe.

3. Once the plug or trap is removed, clean out the trap with your fingers or with a disassembled wire coat hanger.

4. Replace the plug or reattach the trap to the drain pipe, fastening the nuts tightly so that the water does not leak but not so tightly as to damage the threads.

5. Turn on the water to test the drain and check for leaks.

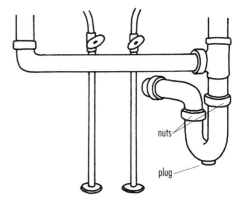

Unscrew the nuts or remove the plug to clean out drain trap.

Using a Sink Auger

Occasionally the clog is further down the pipe. In this case you will need to use a sink auger, also known as a plumber's snake. To assemble the auger, insert the end of the snake-like coil into the auger handle.

1. Place a bucket or shallow tray under the trap to catch any water remaining in the drain.

2. Remove the drain trap with a plumber's wrench by unfastening the two nuts that connect the trap to the drain pipe.

3. Insert the blade of the snake into the pipe that enters the kitchen wall. Allow the snake to run freely into the pipe. When the coil stops running into the pipe, you have reached the blockage or a bend in the pipe.

4. Tighten the screw handle and rotate the auger handle in a clockwise direction. This moves the snake coil around the bend in the pipe or enables it to cut through the blockage.

5. Reattach the drain pipe, turn on the water, and test the drain. This process should take care of the problem.

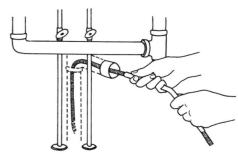

Push the auger in until you feel it hit the stoppage.

Unclogging the Bathroom Sink Drain

Cause	Remedy	Page
Gunk in drain	Use plunger	30
	Clean water stopper	30
	Clean drain trap	31
	Use sink auger	31

Bathroom sinks often become clogged with a combination of hair, grease, and soap, which prevents water from draining properly.

<u>Tools to Have on Hand:</u> plunger, large adjustable wrench (as needed), vise grips (as needed), pipe wrench (as needed)

Plunging the Drain
Try using a plunger first.
1. Fill the sink with about two inches of water.
2. Hold a plunger directly over the drain and plunge down, then pull up hard. Do this several times and then check to see if the water drains.

Cleaning the Water Stopper
Most bathroom sinks have a water stopper built into the fixture, except for older sinks that have removable rubber drain plugs. Underneath the sink and behind the drain pipe, there is a pivot arm that regulates the up-and-down motion of the water stopper. The arm is held in place by a retaining nut (see drawing at left).
1. Unscrew the nut and push the arm toward the back of the sink. This lifts the stopper up from the drain hole.
2. Clean the stopper and the drain with a disassembled coat hanger or some other instrument that will reach into the drain.
3. Reassemble the arm, tighten the retaining nut, and check the drain.

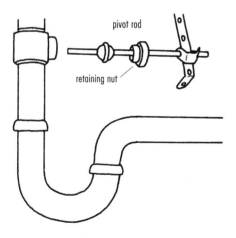

pivot rod

retaining nut

Water stopper

Cleaning the Drain Trap

If that doesn't work, you will have to clean the drain trap. The trap is located under the sink. Some traps have a clean-out plug located at the bottom.

1. Place a pan under the trap to catch the water in the drain pipe.
2. Unscrew the clean-out plug with a large adjustable wrench. If the trap does not have a plug, disassemble the trap with a plumber's wrench. The trap connects two sections of pipe with a large nut screwed onto threaded pipe. Place the wrench around the nut and turn it counterclockwise to loosen it (see drawing at right). Be careful not to damage the threads by applying too much pressure.
3. Once the plug or trap is removed, clean out the trap by hand or with any suitable tool such as an auger or a disassembled coat hanger.
4. Reassemble the drain pipe and plug and test the drain.

Using a Sink Auger

If all the above methods fail, that means the clog is located beyond the drain trap and you will need to attack the problem by inserting a sink auger into the pipe that enters the bathroom wall.

1. Place a bucket or shallow tray under the trap to catch any water remaining in the drain.
2. Remove the drain trap with a pipe wrench by unfastening the nut that connects the trap to the two sections of pipe.
3. Insert the blade of the snake into the pipe that enters the bathroom wall. Allow the snake to run freely into the pipe. When the coil stops running into the pipe, you have reached the blockage or a bend in the pipe.
4. Tighten the screw handle and rotate the auger handle in a clockwise direction. This moves the snake coil around the bend in the pipe or enables it to cut through the blockage.
5. Reattach the drain trap, turn on the water, and test the drain. This process should take care of the problem.

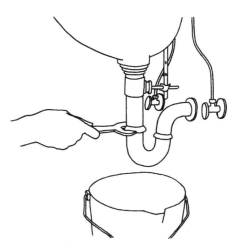

Step 2: You can remove the drain trap to clean it.

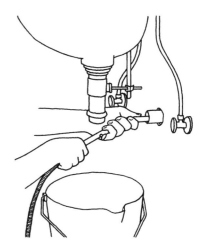

Step 3: Run an auger into the drain pipe until it meets the stoppage.

Unclogging the Toilet

CAUSE	REMEDY	PAGE
Too much paper or foreign object in bowl	Plunge out	32
	Use toilet auger	32
	Call plumber	

<u>Tools to Have on Hand:</u> plunger, wire coat hanger (as needed), toilet auger (as needed)

Plunging

When your toilet becomes stopped up and overflows, first try using a plunger.

1. Turn off the water to the toilet at the shut-off valve near the base.
2. Place the plunger over the hole in the bottom of the toilet bowl.
3. Push down hard and pull up. This action creates a partial vacuum, which should dislodge what is obstructing the flow of waste water. Plunge down in this manner several times.

Using a Toilet Auger

If the obstruction remains, you will need to use a toilet auger. A toilet auger is a hollow cylindrical tube with a handle on the top and a snake that proceeds from the bottom as the handle is turned. The bottom end of the auger curves in a J-like shape. You can also use a wire coat hanger. Straighten the hanger but keep the hook on the end.

1. Insert the auger into the bowl and aim it so that the snake goes into the trap.
2. Turn the auger handle, and the snake will gradually move toward the blockage.

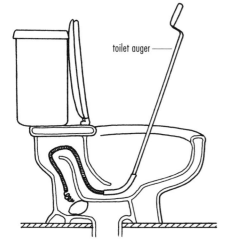

toilet auger

Step 3: Hook the blockage with the auger. Do not push it further into the drain.

3.   When you reach the blockage, try to hook it and force it back into the toilet bowl by pulling down or by turning the auger handle in the opposite direction to pull in the snake. Avoid pushing the obstruction further into the trap.

If after using the auger the blockage still remains, you had better call a plumber. The only solution now is to disassemble the toilet, which is a difficult job.

MAKING IT LAST

Clog Prevention

The best way to avoid calling a plumber is to deal with the clog before it fully develops. If you notice that your toilet fills almost to the top of the tank and drains slowly, a clog is forming. It is much easier to deal with the problem when these symptoms first develop than after the clog has fully formed. At this early stage, a plunger will most likely solve the problem just fine.

Replacing the Toilet Seat

Replacing a cracked, worn, or damaged toilet seat is usually a simple job. The seat is attached to the back of the toilet bowl with nuts and bolts. If you are lucky, the bolts fastening the seat are plastic instead of metal, so they have not rusted in place.

<u>Tools to Have on Hand:</u> straight-slot screwdriver, adjustable wrench, hacksaw (as needed)

1.   With a screwdriver pry up the bolt covers and loosen the bolts. Metal bolts are fastened with a nut on the underside of the bowl. Use a wrench to loosen the nut. If the nut won't budge because it is rusted in place, spray the nut with WD-40 and heat the area with your hair dryer. Try your wrench again. If the nut still won't budge, you will have to cut the bolt in two with a hacksaw, which is a difficult task.

2.   Remove the old toilet seat.

3.   Place the new seat on the bowl and insert the two bolts into the holes in the bowl. Place the nut on the bolt and tighten it down. Don't tighten too much or you may crack the bowl.

4.   After a week, tighten each bolt one more time.

Unclogging the Main Drain

PROBLEM	CAUSE	REMEDY	PAGE
More than one fixture drain clogged	Blockage in the main drain	Use sink auger	34
		Call a plumber	

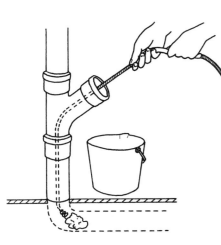

Step 2: Thread a sink auger through the clean-out joint of the main drain.

The drainage system in your house consists of drains for each fixture leading into a main drain, which carries all of the waste out of the house. If two or more drains are clogged, the blockage may be in the main drain.

Before unclogging, be prepared with a mop, towels, and buckets, because there may be several gallons of water backed up in the pipe.

Tools to Have on Hand: pipe wrench, large adjustable wrench (as needed), sink auger

1. In the basement, find a large cast iron or plastic pipe that extends into the ground. About three or four feet from the ground there is a clean-out plug for the main drain, located on a small pipe that forms a Y-shape with the main pipe. Use a pipe or an adjustable wrench to remove the cap to the clean-out plug.

2. Thread a sink auger into the opening and move it toward the sewer. You may need to rent a long, powered auger to reach the blockage. If you succeed in removing the blockage, rinse out the pipe with fresh water from a garden hose. If the blockage remains, call a plumber.

ENERGY SAVER

Hard-to-Find Leaks

A wet area in your yard, a wet spot on the wall or ceiling, or a large water bill all point to a leak somewhere in your plumbing system. If you suspect a leak but can't find it, try this test. Turn off all the water faucets both inside and outside your house. Then go to your water meter and watch the one-cubic-foot dial carefully for at least twenty minutes. If it moves at all, you have a leak that is probably underground or in a wall. Keep the water turned off and call the water company for help. They are usually willing to come to your home at no charge to find the leak.

Repairing or Insulating Pipes

Problem	Cause	Remedy	Page
Water won't run through pipes	Pipes frozen	Thaw out pipes	35
Pipes freeze frequently	Pipes uninsulated and exposed; pipes not adequately insulated	Insulate pipes	35
Pipes leaking	Pipes froze and burst, then thawed	Repair leak	36–37

If your pipes are exposed in the garage, in an uninsulated basement, under the house, or on the side of the house, they may freeze. Even in warmer climates the temperature sometimes dips below freezing.

Insulating Pipes

An easy solution is to cover the pipes with an insulation material. You can purchase foam pipe insulation cut to the diameter of your pipe at a building supply store. With a slit along the side, the insulation is easy to slip onto the pipe. Once the insulation is on the pipe, make sure you seal all the seams tightly with duct tape (see drawing below). Other forms of insulation such as pipe wrap and insulation tape may be less expensive but are not quite as easy to install.

If a pipe or drain does freeze, don't panic and call the plumber. First, listen to the weather forecast for the day. If the temperature rises above 32°F, the pipes may thaw with no damage. There is also the chance that the expansion caused by the water freezing will split the pipe, creating a leak. If you have to leave the house and cannot deal with the problem immediately, turn off the main water valve and flip off the circuit breaker for your water heater and pump, if you have one, so that the water does not thaw and run out through the split in the pipe.

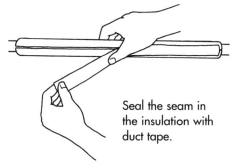

Seal the seam in the insulation with duct tape.

How to Prevent Freezing

The only way to guarantee that the pipes won't freeze in a poorly insulated house is to drain the plumbing system. Short of that solution, try to:

- Insulate exposed pipes. If you don't have pipe insulation, wrap your pipes with towels temporarily.
- Heat areas in your house where pipes are vulnerable. Plug in an electric heater or hang an incandescent light bulb near pipes.
- Open the door of a heated room to an unheated room where pipes are located. If it is really cold, set up an electric fan to blow warm air into the unheated room.
- Keep both hot and cold faucets dripping throughout a cold night. Running water is less likely to freeze.

Repairing Frozen Pipes

To fix the problem immediately, you will need to purchase a pipe cutter and a pipe repair kit at your local hardware store. This wonderful kit contains a plastic section of pipe with washers and pressure nuts on each side. Neither the pipe cutter nor the repair kit is expensive. Another option is to go to the local car parts store and buy a length of heater tubing with an opening that will fit snugly on your pipe. You will also need two clamps. They are tightened with a screwdriver and come in various sizes according to the tubing size.

<u>Tools to Have on Hand:</u> hair dryer, pipe cutter, straight-slot screwdriver

1. Turn off the main water valve.

2. To locate the problem, examine all exposed pipes for a bulge or split.

3. Once you locate the problem spot or spots, turn on all the faucets that are blocked so that when you heat the pipe, the vapor from the melting ice can escape. If there is nowhere for the vapor to go, the pipe might burst.

4. Use a hair dryer to heat the spot. Soon the pipe should start to thaw. If the pipe is broken, it will begin to drip and you will know where to repair it.

5. Repeat this process at all places where there is a definite bulge or split.

6. Cut away the broken section of pipe with a pipe cutter. Slip the pipe cutter over the pipe and tighten slightly by turning the adjusting knob. Rotate the cutter around the pipe until it turns easily. Tighten the cutter again slightly and rotate. Repeat this procedure until the pipe breaks off. Do not tighten the cutter too much at a time or it will not work properly and you may end up bending or denting the pipe. Cut out only the split or deformed section.

7. Slip the two pressure nuts onto the pipe ends facing each other.

8. Insert the washers onto the ends of each pipe and slip the repair piece onto each pipe end.

9. Tighten the pressure nuts at each end of the repair piece and you are finished.

10. If you are using heater tubing, cut the tube the size of the cut in your pipe and allow for two inches on either side. Slip the clamps on the

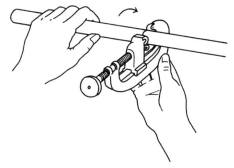

Step 6: Use a pipe cutter to cut away the broken section of pipe.

pressure nut

Step 7: Slip the two pressure nuts onto the pipe ends.

Blocking Water

If water continues to run out pipe, wad up a piece of white bread and stuff it into the pipe. The bread disintegrates.

tubing and push each end onto the pipe. Take a screwdriver and tighten the clamps at either end of the pipe, making sure that the clamps are on the pipe.

11. Once you have completed the job, turn the water back on and see what happens. If there is no evidence of leaks, go upstairs and see if the water is running where it had been previously blocked. If it is not running, there are still frozen places in the pipe. Keep at it.

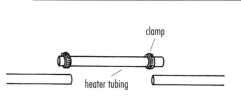

Step 10: Slip the clamps onto the tubing and the overlapping ends onto the pipe. Tighten the clamps.

Winterizing Your Plumbing

To prepare an unwinterized house such as a vacation home for cold weather, you must winterize the plumbing.

1. First turn off the main water valve (see pages 8–9). If you receive your water from a public utility, the utility will need to shut off the main water valve outside your house.

2. Turn on all the spigots in the house, beginning on the top floor and working down. Make sure to get them all.

3. Flush all toilets and pour about two cups of household antifreeze into each toilet trap.

4. Pour antifreeze into the sink and bathtub traps. These traps should not be drained because they keep noxious odors and vermin from entering your home.

5. Put antifreeze in the main trap in the basement by unscrewing the clean-out plug and pouring in the antifreeze.

6. Turn off the power to the water heater at the circuit breaker box. Drain the water heater by attaching a garden hose to the drain valve. Make sure the hose is pointing downhill and outside the house.

7. Open the outdoor spigot, turn off the water, and take off the hose. It's a good idea to drain the water in your hose by hanging it downhill to prevent the water from freezing and cracking the hose. If you want to be sure that water in the pipe leading to the spigot won't freeze, have a plumber install a shut-off valve in your garage with a bleeder valve. Once installed, turn off the water to the pipe and open the bleeder valve. This forces air through the pipe, which cleans out any remaining water.

Chapter Two

2

Electricity

AT A GLANCE

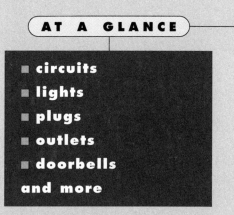

- circuits
- lights
- plugs
- outlets
- doorbells

and more

Electricity Basics

Many people find electrical problems scary. Although there are sound reasons to have a healthy respect for your electrical system, its operation is quite easy to understand. Once you understand how your system works and after taking the important precaution of turning off the power and testing the circuit with a voltage probe, you can confidently fix a number of simple electrical problems on your own. However, it's wise to leave the more complicated tasks to an electrician.

Electrical power from a utility company comes into your home through a meter that monitors your consumption. From there it proceeds to a circuit breaker or fuse box, which channels the electrical energy into circuits (circular pathways) that are distributed throughout your house.

Each area of a home has a corresponding circuit or fuse. To shut off the flow of electricity to a particular area, turn off the appropriate circuit in the circuit breaker or remove the corresponding fuse in the fuse box in the basement. The fuses or breakers should be labeled in the box according to the sections of the house they cover. If they are unmarked, it is important to find out what circuit or fuse governs the electricity in each area of your home.

Home electrical system

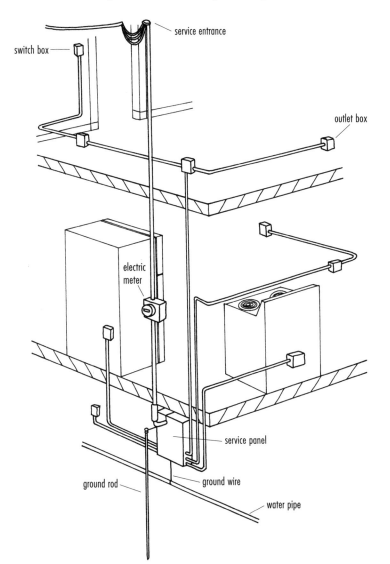

- service entrance
- switch box
- outlet box
- electric meter
- service panel
- ground rod
- ground wire
- water pipe

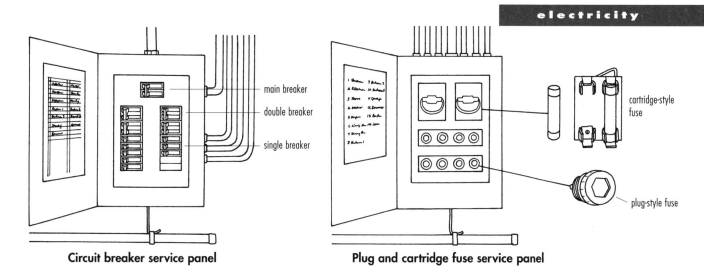

Circuit breaker service panel	**Plug and cartridge fuse service panel**

Labels for circuit breaker service panel: main breaker, double breaker, single breaker

Labels for plug and cartridge fuse service panel: cartridge-style fuse, plug-style fuse

Get a friend to help you determine what breaker or fuse turns each area of the house on or off. If you are alone, plug a radio into an outlet and turn the circuit breakers off or remove fuses one at a time. Be careful not to insert anything into the empty fuse holder. When the radio goes off, you know that is the circuit for that outlet. There is usually more than one outlet for each circuit, except in the case of a large appliance, which can use one or two circuits by itself. Mark the location of the circuit or fuse on your box immediately.

SAFETY TIP

Sensing Current Leaks

A ground fault circuit interrupter (GFCI) is a device that senses tiny leakages of current. When it detects a leak, it immediately turns off the power before any harm is done. Standard electrical code requires GFCI's for bathrooms, garages, and outdoor receptacles. They are not required in basements or shops, places where you might be using power tools and other types of electrical equipment. If you happen to be in a position of providing a good ground for errant electricity, like standing on a wet basement floor, you are vulnerable to shock, which can be fatal. With this in mind, it would be a good idea to purchase a plug-in GFCI. You simply plug it into a receptacle and then plug your tool or appliance into the GFCI. It's a simple precaution that could save your life.

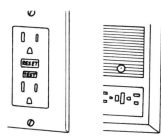

permanent receptacle type GFCI	portable plug-in type GFCI

Ground fault circuit interrupters (GFCI) sense tiny leakages of current.

What to Do When the Power Goes Off

PROBLEM	CAUSE	REMEDY	PAGE
Power goes off in one area	Overloaded circuit	Unplug appliances and turn on circuit breaker or replace blown fuse	42
	Short circuit	Unplug damaged cords and turn on circuit breaker or replace blown fuse	43
		Call an electrician	

Sometimes a circuit turns off automatically or a fuse blows. This happens because the circuit breaker or the fuse box is a safety device to prevent fire from occurring from the overloading or shorting of electric circuits in your house. When this happens, you must determine if the problem is from an overloaded circuit or a short circuit. The general rule is that an overloaded circuit will take several seconds or a minute to blow, while a short circuit will trip the circuit immediately.

Overloaded Circuit

If you plug in too many appliances in one area, the circuit breaker or fuse box will automatically shut off the electric current to that area of the house.

Tools to Have on Hand: voltage tester, flashlight

1. When the power goes off, go to the service panel and look inside (see drawings on page 41). In a circuit breaker system, if the switch to that area of the house is between the *on* and *off* position, go back and unplug all appliances in that location. For fuse boxes, look inside the box and you will see glass-topped fuses. A blown fuse will have a broken wire or blackened top. Unplug all appliances in the area of the house that the blown fuse services.

2. When you have made sure that the circuit is not overloaded, flip the circuit breaker to the *off* position and then to the *on* position or replace the blown fuse by unscrewing the broken one and replacing it with a fuse of equal amperage. (The number is printed on the top of the fuse.)

3. When you have returned power to the particular area of your home, plug each appliance in one at a time. This method will enable you to determine the load capacity of the circuit. If the first appliance turned on triggers the circuit breaker or blows the fuse, then you have a serious problem that will require the services of an electrician.

Short Circuit

1. If you suspect a short circuit, check all the cords and plugs for exposed or frayed wires.

2. If you discover a problem, try the circuit again or replace the fuse, leaving the lamp or appliance with the damaged cord unplugged. If that solves the problem, repair or replace the device. If the circuit fails again, the short may be in the house wiring, which will require calling an electrician to fix.

The Main Power Switch

One main switch controls all the electricity in the house. This switch is usually located at the top of the circuit breaker (see drawing on page 41). If you are fixing something electrical and do not know which circuit controls that area of the house, just flip the main switch to *off* to turn off all the electricity in your house.

Timing Turn-Offs

If you need to shut off power frequently to an area of your home to conserve energy, it is a good idea to purchase a timing switch for that area. Ask a reputable electrician about this practical device. The water heater is the appliance that most often requires a timing switch.

Flashlight
Because serivce panels are often in dark places, keep a flashlight with rechargeable batteries nearby.

Repairing Incandescent Light Fixtures

PROBLEM	CAUSE	REMEDY	PAGE
Light doesn't work	Light bulb burned out	Replace bulb	45
	Loose or broken wires	Repair and tighten wires	45
	Light switch broken	Replace light switch	50–51
	Blown fuse	Repair wires	45
	Socket defective	Replace socket	46
Light flickers	Light bulb loose	Tighten bulb	46
	Wire coating melted	Tape wire	46
	Socket defective	Replace socket	46
	Dimmer switch	Replace dimmer switch	52

Incandescent light bulbs are the most common, popular, and least expensive light bulbs. You find them most frequently used in household lamps and light fixtures. They are popular because they provide a soft, warm light that is gentle on the eyes. High-intensity incandescent bulbs generate large amounts of light and are used for search and flood lights located outside the home.

Incandescent bulbs operate with a thin tungsten wire, or filament, placed inside a bulb. When electricity moves through the tungsten filament, it glows with light and heat. Over time the filament becomes thinner and slowly oxidizes. As this process occurs, the filament gives off tiny black particles that create a black film on the bulb. At some point the filament becomes too thin and breaks and the bulb burns out.

Incandescent light fixtures operate much the same as table lamps do: wire leads connect the socket to the house wiring system. If the light does not work, the problem may be as simple as a burned out light bulb. Or you may need to repair the fixture. It is also possible that the light switch has gone bad and needs replacing (see page 50).

Changing the Bulb

If the bulb rattles when you shake it, it has indeed burned out. When replacing the bulb, check to be sure that the maximum recommended wattage of the fixture is not lower than the bulb you are using. The wattage is usually indicated on the part that holds the socket. Because many fixtures do not allow for proper air circulation, they get hotter than lamps. Bulbs that exceed the maximum wattage recommendation generate too much heat, which can melt the wire insulation and cause a dangerous short circuit.

Repairing the Wires in the Fixture

<u>Tools to Have on Hand:</u> straight-slot screwdriver

1. Turn off the power to the fixture at the circuit breaker and test the circuit with a voltage tester.

2. Remove the cover and plate that hold the fixture to the ceiling or wall. Disassemble the fixture. Be careful not to drop the cover and note how the parts fit together so that you can reassemble them later.

3. Once you have uncovered the electrical box, you will probably see three (sometimes two) wires attached to the socket mechanism. The black one is the hot wire that carries the current from the circuit breaker to the fixture. The white wire takes the used current back to the breaker, where it is safely guided into the earth outside your house.

Trouble can arise, however, when a short circuit is created that causes current to leak to adjacent metal parts. These parts become "hot" and will shock you if touched because your body serves as the path the current travels to the ground. For safety reasons, most fixtures provide a third wire, either green or bare, which grounds the equipment (see drawing on page 46).

4. Check for loose or broken wires connected to the socket and tighten all connections. If you find a damaged wire, peel back the insulation and resplice the wire by twisting the ends together. Cover them carefully with electrical tape (see page 54).

SAFETY TIP

Handling Hot Light Bulbs

Be careful with hot light bulbs. Protect your hands if you have to handle them.

SAFETY TIP

Fire Hazard

To protect against fire, provide light bulbs with plenty of space. They need air circulation to cool down. They also should never be placed near combustible curtains or other like materials.

Each light fixture comes with an allowable wattage. Do not use bulbs that exceed that wattage because it will lead to dangerous overheating.

With the power turned off, use a continuity tester to test the socket.

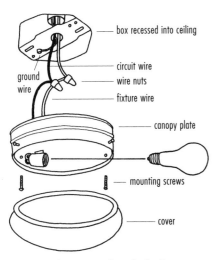

box recessed into ceiling

circuit wire

ground wire

wire nuts

fixture wire

canopy plate

mounting screws

cover

Incandescent ceiling light fixture

Testing the Socket

In cases where the fixture blows a fuse or trips a circuit, look first for cut or frayed wires. If you find any, turn off the power at the circuit breaker and repair the wire as described on page 45. You will also need to test the socket. With the power turned off, use a continuity tester to test the socket (see page 177). If the light on the tester does not turn on, the socket is defective.

Some sockets are easily disassembled and replaced, while others are impossible and will require that you purchase a new fixture.

Fixing a Flickering Bulb

A flickering light may be caused by a loose light bulb.

1. Check and secure the bulb.

2. If the bulb is secure, turn off the power and check for melted insulation on the wires. If you find a wire with melted insulation, tape it.

3. If that doesn't work, the socket may be defective. Follow the instructions above to test the socket. If it is defective, replace it.

4. Finally, the dimmer switch may be causing the flickering. To replace the switch, follow the instructions on page 52.

Installing a New Lighting Fixture

A good way to change the appearance of a room is to replace an old lighting fixture. In most cases, this job is more cumbersome than difficult.

<u>Tools to Have on Hand:</u> straight-slot or Phillips screwdriver, small knife

1. Turn off the power to the light at the circuit breaker. It is not enough to merely turn off the wall switch. Power may remain in the white and ground wires, which can shock you.

2. Take off the bulb cover and remove the light bulb.

3. Next, unfasten any screws holding the light fixture to the ceiling. The fixture should now detach from the ceiling.

4. Disconnect the wires that connect the old fixture to the box.

5. There are two basic ways of attaching fixtures to the ceiling. One uses screws to bolt a strap to the ceiling. The second has a stud that comes down from the center of the box and attaches to a hickey (see drawings at right). Follow the instructions that come with your new fixture.

6. Assuming that the old bracket will accommodate the new fixture, strip ¾ of an inch off the insulation of the black, white, and green wires of the new fixture. To strip the insulation, take a small knife and gently cut around the wire coating, making sure that you do not cut into the wire itself. Slip the coating off.

7. Raise the new fixture and connect the black, white, and grounding wires to the corresponding wires in the box and fasten them together with wire nuts. Tape the wire nuts to make sure they stay on.

8. Secure the fixture to the support mechanism and put the light bulb into place. Now you can turn on the power to see if the fixture works.

9. If so, refasten the bulb cover and the project is complete.

If the light does not come on, first test the light bulb. Next, check the wiring to make sure the connections are securely fastened and that the wires are connected black to black, white to white, and ground to ground. If you see a problem with the wiring, make sure to turn the power off at the circuit breaker before attempting to fix it. Finally, the new fixture may itself be faulty and need to be exchanged.

Installing Swag Lighting

It is possible to add lighting to a room without installing a new fixture. A swag light consists of an electric cord with a plug on one end and a socket and shade on the other end. The package comes with two hooks that attach to the ceiling.

<u>Tool to Have on Hand:</u> straight-slot screwdriver

Place the first hook where the fixture is to be located. It is best to screw the hook into a ceiling joist because the hook must support the weight of the lamp. If there is no joist near where you plan to locate the lamp, use a toggle bolt (see page 125) to support the lamp. Install the second hook as near to the wall as possible. Its purpose is to direct the electric cord to an outlet. Now all you do is plug in your new light.

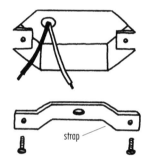

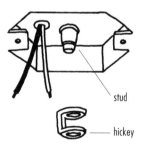

Ceiling fixtures may be mounted with either a strap or a hickey.

Fluorescent Lighting

PROBLEM	CAUSE	REMEDY	PAGE
Burned-out tube	Loose wire or broken connection	Repair wire and tighten connection; replace tube	48–49
Flickering tube	Starter not sitting properly in fixture	Adjust starter	49
	Faulty starter	Replace starter	49
Humming tube or acrid smell	Faulty ballast	Replace fixture or ballast	49

Fluorescent lighting provides more uniform illumination than does incandescent lighting and is far more energy efficient. Because the design of fluorescent fixtures is limited by the shape of the tubes, these lights are most often found in informal spaces like kitchens, basements, and family rooms.

There are two types of fluorescent lights. One has a starter built into the tube and the other requires a starter in the fixture to operate properly. All fluorescent lights have a ballast, a small rectangular box with wires running through it. It functions as a transformer by reducing the flow of electricity into the tube. As electricity enters the tube, it excites gas inside the tube, which glows with a cool, diffused light. Fluorescent lights use less electricity and produce less heat than incandescent bulbs, which allows the tubes to last far longer.

Burned-Out Tube

Fluorescent tubes usually do not burn out abruptly. Here are some things to try if yours fails to operate.

Tool to Have on Hand: straight-slot screwdriver (as needed)

1. If your light goes out suddenly, wiggle the ends of the tube to make sure it is sitting properly in the fixture.

2. If that doesn't work, the problem may involve a loose wire or broken connection. Turn off the power to the light at the circuit breaker.

3. Now you can remove the fixture cover and tubes. Inspect all wire connections and tighten any loose ones. (See drawing on page 49.)

Replacing a Fluorescent Tube

A fixture that provides only partial light may require a new tube. A tube that blinks or has blackened ends is beginning to fail and should be replaced.

1. Turn off the light.
2. Press the tube in and turn it counterclockwise ¼ to ½ inch and pull it out.
3. Replace the tube with a new one of the same wattage.

Flickering Tube

Older fixtures require a separate starter, which causes the tube to flicker as it lights up.

1. If the light continues to flicker, check to see that the starter, the small tube about 1¼ inches long and ¾ inch wide, is sitting properly in the fixture by pushing it in and turning it clockwise. If the ends of the tube light up but the center does not, the starter needs to be replaced.
2. Remove the starter by pressing it in and turning it counterclockwise with a ¼ to ½ turn, and then pull it out.
3. Take the old starter to an electrical supply store and replace it.

Replacing the Ballast

A humming sound or an acrid smell indicates that the ballast is going bad. Before replacing it, compare the price of a new ballast with the price of a new fixture. You may save no money by replacing the ballast.
<u>Tools to Have on Hand:</u> straight-slot or Phillips screwdriver (as needed)

1. If you decide to replace the ballast, turn off the power at the circuit breaker first.
2. Next, remove the tubes and starter. There will be a cover over the ballast. Covers are either screwed on or have a simple latch mechanism.
3. Remove the cover and you will see the ballast and the wires connected to it. The tube holders will probably have to be replaced also.
4. Remove the ballast and tube holders and take them to an electrical supply store. Replace them with identical parts.
5. Resecure the ballast, tube holders, starters, and tubes, and turn the power back on. That should fix your problem.

Fluorescent light fixture

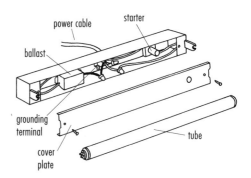

power cable · starter · ballast · grounding terminal · cover plate · tube

---

SAFETY TIP

Handling Broken Fluorescent Tubes

Fluorescent tubes contain mercury, which is a highly toxic chemical. If the tube breaks, do not handle it with your bare hands.

Electrical Switches, Cords, Plugs, and Outlets

PROBLEM	CAUSE	REMEDY	PAGE
Light switch does not go on	Circuit breaker off	Turn on circuit breaker	50
	Bulb burned out	Replace bulb	45
	Faulty light switch	Replace switch	50–51
Outlet does not work		Replace outlet	53
Electrical cord or plug emits shock	Frayed cord or faulty plug	Repair cord; replace plug	53–54

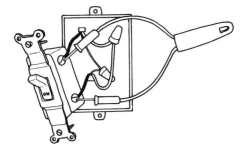

Use a neon tester to determine whether the switch is at fault.

Replacing Electrical Switches

If you enter a room, flip the light switch, and nothing happens, one of the following could be wrong:

• The **circuit breaker may be off** for that part of the house. Check to see if the other electrical units in the room are working. If the light you switched *on* is the only thing not working, replace the bulb.

• The bulb may have burned out.

• The **switch may be defective.** If the light still does not work after replacing the bulb, test the switch. If you have a neon tester, you can do this before heading to the hardware store. Take off the switch cover with a screwdriver. Next take your neon tester and touch its probes to the terminal screws with the switch in the *on* position (see drawing at left). Be careful not to let the probes touch the box sides. If the tester lights, the switch needs replacing.

Tools to Have on Hand: neon tester, straight-slot screwdriver

To replace the switch, proceed as follows:

1. Turn off the power to the switch at the circuit breaker.

2. Remove the switch cover with a screwdriver and you will see two screws holding the switch in place on the wall.

3. Remove these screws and pull the switch out of the wall. You will now see two wires connected to the switch. They will either be attached to two screws on the sides of the switch or they will be inserted into the back of the switch.

4. Loosen the screws and disconnect the wires or gently pull the wires out of the back of the switch. Note where the wires were attached because you will repeat this procedure in reverse order when you reconnect the new switch. The switch will now be free.

5. Take this switch to a hardware or electrical supply store and replace it with a similar switch.

6. Reconnect the new switch to the wires in the wall, screw it back onto the wall, replace the cover, and turn the power back on. Your problem should now be solved.

Replacing a Three-Way Switch

In the event that you are dealing with a three-way switch, the same principles apply. The name three-way switch is a little misleading because such a switch controls lights from two locations, not three. The basic principle is that the common or hot wire (the dark-colored one) proceeds from the power source to the first switch. Two lighter-colored traveler wires link the two switches together. The common wire then runs from the second switch to the light fixture. A white wire runs from the power source to the light fixture, which completes the circuit.

All that you need to remember is to make a wire diagram before unfastening the wires to the damaged switch. Install the new three-way switch with the same wiring pattern that you found in the damaged switch.

Dimmer Switches

Lights can be strategically placed to highlight a particular piece of furniture or a specific area of a room. Bright lights make a room look cheerful while dim lights create a sense of intimacy and relaxation.

Installing a dimmer switch allows you to control the amount of illumination a light puts out. These switches also help to conserve energy and increase the life of your light bulb because a dimmed filament burns at a lower temperature, which slows the burn-out process. It is important to note that dimmer switches can only be used to control lighting — not appliances or the functioning of an electrical outlet. Also, incandescent and fluorescent lights require different types of dimmer switches.

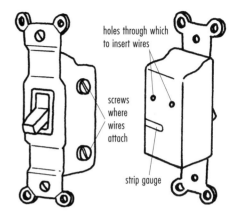

holes through which to insert wires

screws where wires attach

strip gauge

Two kinds of light switches

Diagramming Wires
Make a wiring diagram before unfastening the wires. It will help you to reattach the wires when you install the new switch.

Tool to Have on Hand: straight-slot screwdriver

Installing Incandescent Dimmer Switches. Installing an incandescent dimmer switch is really a simple project. You install it the same way you install any lighting switch.

1. Turn off the power to the switch at the circuit breaker.
2. Remove the switch cover with a screwdriver and you will see two screws holding the switch in place on the wall.

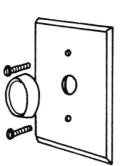
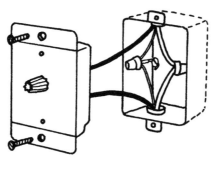

3. Remove these screws and pull the switch out of the wall. You will now see two wires connected to the switch. They will either be attached to two screws on the side of the switch or they will be inserted into the back of the switch.

4. Loosen the screws and disconnect the wires or press a small screwdriver against the release slot on the switch and pull out the wires. Note where the wires were attached because you will repeat this procedure in reverse order when you reconnect the dimmer switch. The old switch will now be free.

Installing a dimmer switch

5. Take this switch to a hardware or electrical supply store and replace it with a suitable dimmer switch.

6. Reconnect the dimmer switch to the wires in the wall, screw it back onto the wall, replace the cover, and turn the power back on.

If you are dealing with a three-way switch, it is best to install only one dimming switch and to leave the other switch alone. Make sure you attach the black wire from the box (the common wire) to the black switch wire. Then connect the two red wires from the switch (the traveler wires) to the traveler wires in the box — one will likely be red and the other white.

Installing Fluorescent Dimmer Switches. Fluorescent dimmer switches are installed in the same way as incandescent dimmer switches with one exception. You must install a special ballast, which you can purchase at an electrical supply store.

Replacing an Outlet

Replacing an outlet is similar to replacing a switch. The obvious test for an outlet is to plug in an electrical appliance that you know works.

Tool to Have on Hand: straight-slot screwdriver

1. Turn off the power to the outlet at the circuit breaker box. Test the circuit with a voltage tester to be sure the power is off.

2. Next remove the outlet cover with a screwdriver. Take the two screws out of the outlet to remove it from the wall and notice how the wires are connected. These wires will be connected to two screws on the sides of the outlet, or will be fastened on the back of the receptacle.

3. Loosen the screws and remove the wires, or depress the release slot in the outlet to free up the wires.

4. Take the old outlet to the hardware store and replace it with a new one just like the old one.

5. Install the new outlet by reversing the above steps. Put the cover back on and turn on the power. Now try testing the appliance again.

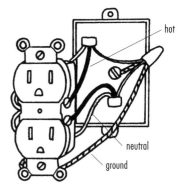

hot

neutral

ground

Outlet at the middle of the circuit

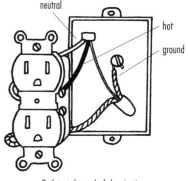

neutral

hot

ground

Outlet at the end of the circuit

Replacing an outlet

Replacing Plugs

If the problem with the cord is in the plug, there are several options.

Molded Rubber Plugs. For molded rubber plugs, unplug the light, cut the plug off and bring it to the hardware store to be replaced. Purchase the type of plug that can be clamped back onto the cord.

Two-Pronged Plugs.

1. Unplug the appliance and cut off the plug. Purchase a plug that can be attached to the two wire strands with screws.

2. Thread the wire into the plug, separate the two strands, and strip the insulation material.

3. Tie the two strands into a loop before connecting them to the screws. Loosen the screws and wind a small part of the wire around the screw.

4. Tighten the screws and cover them with the insulating material that comes with the plug.

Three-Wire Extension Cords. For three-wire extension cords, replace the three-pronged plug the same way as you would replace a two-pronged plug (above).

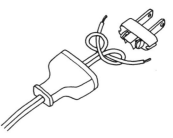

Connecting wires to a new plug

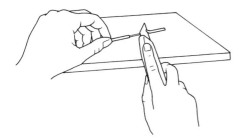

Step 3: To repair a broken wire, peel back the insulation around it, being careful not to cut the wire itself.

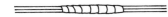

Steps 5–6: Splice wires together by first twisting together the pairs of wires from each section of cord, cover each splice with electrical tape, and then cover the entire splice with tape.

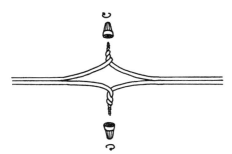

Step 7: Spliced wires may also be reconnected with wire nuts; fasten the nuts securely.

Repairing Cords

Have you ever been shocked? It was probably due to a faulty electrical cord or plug. Rabbits, puppies, and mice love to chew cords, which exposes the wire and interrupts the flow of electricity. With plugs, problems arise when they are yanked out by their cords or stepped on. It is important that you fix these problems, because in addition to causing shocks, they pose fire hazards.

<u>Tools to Have on Hand:</u> kitchen knife, wire stripper (optional), electrical tape, wire nuts (optional), straight-slot screwdriver (as needed)

1. If you discover a frayed cord, unplug the cord and find a sharp kitchen knife.

2. Cut the cord on either side of the damaged wire. Next cut each of the two sections of cord down the middle about two inches.

3. You will now have four strands of wire. You next have to strip off about one inch of the plastic coating that insulates each of the four strands of wire. To do this, take a knife and gently go around the coating of the wire, making sure that you don't cut through the wire.

4. Once this is accomplished, simply slip off the coating, leaving the wire exposed. You can also purchase a wire stripper at the hardware store — an inexpensive and handy tool.

5. To reconnect the two sections of cord, you will have to splice the wires. Take a strand of wire from each section of the cord and twist them together. Do this again to reconnect the remaining wires.

6. Next, take shiny electrical tape and completely cover each set of spliced wires individually with the tape. Then cover the entire section with tape.

7. Another solution is to connect the wires with wire nuts. This is usually the simplest method. Twist the wires together and then insert them into the nut. It is important to make sure that the nut is securely fastened.

Taping Wire
Wrap the tape so that no copper wire is exposed or touching another exposed area. Otherwise, a short will occur.

Repairing a Faulty Doorbell

PROBLEM	CAUSE	REMEDY	PAGE
Doesn't ring	Faulty button	Replace button	55
	Bell contact points corroded	Clean bell contact points	55
	Loose wires	Tighten connections	55
	Faulty transformer	Replace transformer	55–56
	Faulty circuit wire	Call electrician	56
	Faulty bell	Replace bell	56

The good news about repairing a doorbell or chimes is that the voltage for these circuits is so low that you don't have to worry about getting shocked. Electrical power proceeds from your circuit breaker to a transformer, which reduces the power from 120 volts to between 6 and 30 volts. From the transformer, an open circuit is created. When you press the doorbell, the circuit closes and the bell rings (see drawing at right). <u>Tools to Have on Hand:</u> straight-slot screwdriver, volt-ohm meter

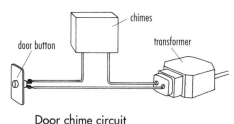

Door chime circuit

The Button

1. Unscrew the button mechanism from the outside door and place a wire or screwdriver across the terminals (see drawing at right). If the bell rings, the button needs to be replaced.

2. If the bell does not ring, clean off the contact points for the button. Contact points for bells located outside the house are often corroded.

3. Check to make sure that all wire connections are tightly fastened. Press the button again and see if the bell rings. If not, check the transformer.

The Transformer

The transformer is usually located near the circuit breaker box or near the door itself. Before testing it, make sure that the wires are firmly attached. Then test the transformer with a volt-ohm meter. Disconnect the wires leading from the chimes to the transformer and touch each terminal of

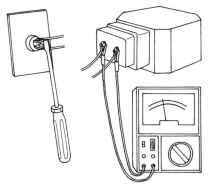

Test the button by placing a screwdriver across the terminals (left). If the bell does not ring, test the transformer with a volt-ohm meter (right). If the meter does not register, replace the transformer.

the transformer with the volt-ohm meter's probes. If the volt-ohm doesn't register, the transformer needs to be replaced.

1. Shut off the power at the circuit breaker box. Test a receptacle on the circuit with a voltage tester to make sure the power is off. In this case you will be working with wires with the normal 120 volts.

2. Once the power is off, you can safely unscrew the transformer and disconnect the wires. There are several different kinds of transformers, so it is important to take the old one to the hardware store so that it can be replaced exactly.

3. Install the new transformer, turn the power back on, and test your doorbell again.

The Bell

If the problem persists, you will need to check the bell itself.

1. With the power shut off at the circuit breaker box, disconnect the bell and clean all the contact points.

2. Make sure that all wire connections are tightly fastened.

3. Test your system again.

4. If you still get no ring, test the bell by hooking it up directly to the transformer. If the bell rings, the problem is probably with the wire that forms the circuit. Replacing the wire is a difficult task that will require the services of an electrician.

5. If the bell doesn't ring, replace the bell and the problem should be fixed.

Faulty Lamp

PROBLEM	CAUSE	REMEDY	PAGE
Lamp does not turn on	Bulb burned out	Replace bulb	57
	Damaged cord	Repair cord	57
	Faulty switch	Replace switch	57

If a lamp fails to turn on, begin by checking the simple things that can go wrong. First check the light bulb. Next check to see that electricity is getting to the outlet by plugging in a lamp or a small appliance that you know works. Finally, check the lamp cord to see if the wires have been cut or damaged, which could interrupt the flow of electricity to the lamp.

Replacing a Broken Lamp Switch

If all of the above check out, the problem with your lamp is probably a worn-out switch.

<u>Tool to Have on Hand:</u> straight-slot screwdriver

1. To replace the switch, begin by unplugging the lamp.
2. Next take the shade off and unscrew the light bulb.
3. To get to the socket and switch, push hard on the outer metal shell of the socket and pull off the shell and insulating jacket together.
4. The next step is to pull the switch out of the lamp (the wire feeds up through the bottom of the lamp). Note that there is a screw on either side of the socket, each one with a wire attached. Unscrew the screws, disconnect the wires, and remove the switch from the socket.
5. Take the switch to the hardware store and replace it.
6. The new switch can be installed by reversing these directions. It does not matter which wires attach to each screw. However, make sure that you loop the wire onto the screw in a clockwise direction because that is the way the screw goes in. Your lamp should now be fixed.

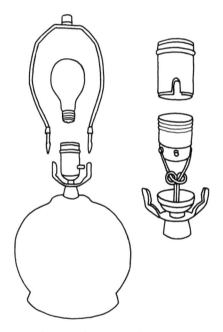

Replacing a lamp switch

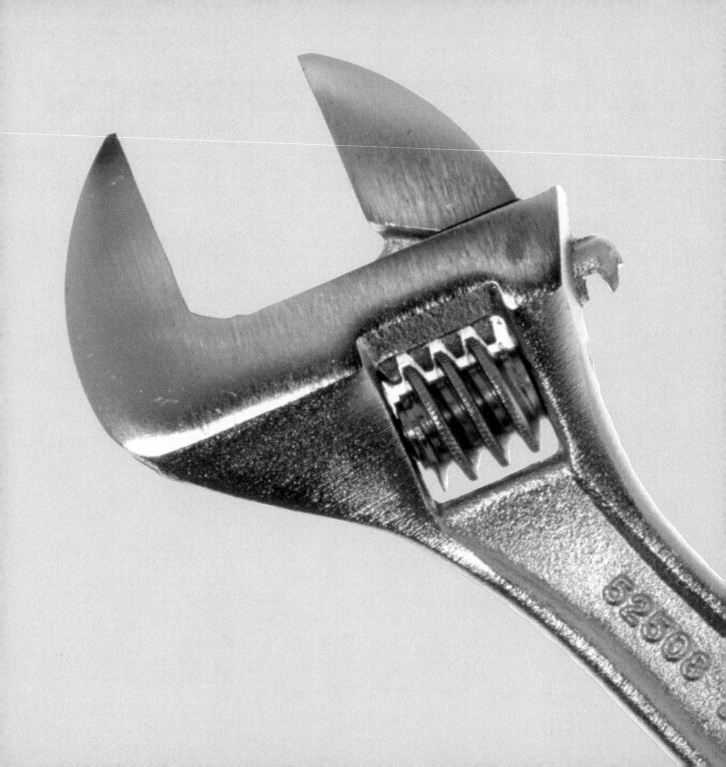

Chapter Three

3

Appliances

AT A GLANCE

- washing machines
- dishwashers
- refrigerators
- vacuum cleaners

and more

If you have an electrical appliance that malfunctions, never call for professional help until you have checked a few simple things: Is the machine plugged in? Did you set the controls properly? Has the breaker tripped or the fuse blown? If so, flip the breaker back on or replace the fuse. If it blows again, the circuit may be overloaded. Unplug the appliance and try the circuit another time. If the problem occurs again, you have a short circuit somewhere and should call an electrician. If the circuit works, plug in the appliance again. If the circuit blows instantly, you may have a short in the appliance and should call a professional. If the circuit works for 10 minutes or all day and then blows, you may have a weak breaker; call an electrician.

Washing Machine

PROBLEM	CAUSE	REMEDY	PAGE
Not agitating	Loose or broken drive belt	Tighten or replace drive belt	61–62
Vibrating	Unbalanced	Redistribute wash load	62
	Not level	Adjust height; check floor	62
Not filling or slowly filling with water	Hose screen clogged	Unclog screen	62–63
	Pipes clogged	Call plumber	63
	Kink in hose	Straighten hose	63
Water does not drain	Drain blocked	Remove blockage	63
	Loose or damaged hose	Tighten clamp or replace hose	63
	Cracked agitator	Replace agitator	64
Machine leaks	Object in basket	Remove object	64
Machine damaging clothes	Rough edges on basket	Call service person to replace basket	64

A washing machine contains three systems: plumbing, electrical, and mechanical. The plumbing system brings in and distributes water throughout the machine. The electrical system directs the machine's operation through control switches, timer, motor, and solenoids. The mechanical system provides cleaning action through the drive belt, agitator, and tub.

Solving Agitating Problems

If your machine is filling with water but not agitating, in some machines the drive belt may be loose or broken. But not all models have drive belts. If you do not find a belt, call a professional to solve the problem.

<u>Tools to Have on Hand</u>: straight-slot or Phillips screwdriver, small adjustable wrench

The drive belt is accessible through either the back panel or the bottom of the appliance, depending on the machine. To expose the bottom of the machine, you will need a strong friend to help you lay the machine face down on the floor.

1. Whether removing the back panel or turning your machine over, make sure to first unplug the machine, shut off the water faucets, and detach the water inlet hoses. (If you are turning your machine over, cover the floor with newspapers in case the transmission leaks oil.)

2. The drive belt runs in a circular direction, connecting the motor with several other parts (see drawing on page 62). Place your thumb on the belt and press in. If the belt indents more than half an inch, it is too loose. If the belt is broken, you will need to call a repairperson.

3. A belt can be tightened by pushing out one of the wheels it is connected to. Find the closest wheel (not connected to the motor); find the adjusting bolt near it.

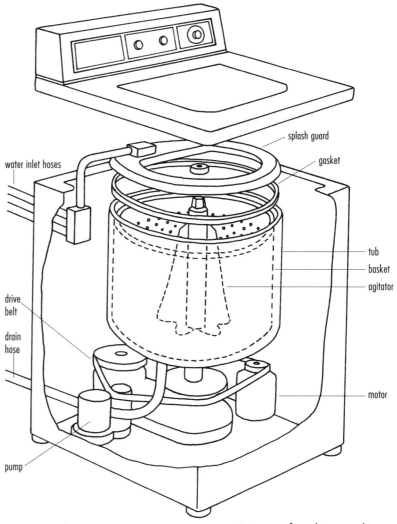

Cutaway of washing machine

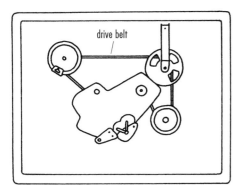

The drive belt is accessible either at the back or on the bottom of your machine.

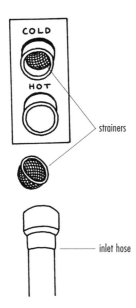

Examine the screens and hoses for stoppages.

4. Loosen the bolt just enough so that the wheel slides, but make sure the bolt remains in the hole.

5. Push the wheel out as far as possible and then tighten the bolt so that the wheel maintains its new position. This should tighten the belt enough to agitate your machine.

6. If not, the motor or transmission is faulty and will require the work of a professional service person.

Fixing Vibrating Washing Machine

When your machine vibrates excessively in the spin cycle, it is probably unbalanced.

<u>Tools to Have on Hand:</u> vise grips (as needed), level

First redistribute the wash load. If the machine continues to vibrate, it may not be level. Use a level and adjust the washer's height by turning the leveling feet at the bottom of the machine either in or out. When the machine is level, be sure to lock the lock nut on the leveling feet.

Vibrating can also be caused by a weak floor. Inspect the floor under the washer and call a carpenter if the floor needs additional support.

Water Problems with Washing Machine

If your machine is filling with water very slowly, check to make sure that the faucets on the wall are fully turned on. If they are and the connecting hoses are not kinked, one or both of the hoses may be blocked. At the end of each water hose there is a small screen that can get clogged with residue and deposits in the water.

<u>Tool to Have on Hand:</u> vise grips (as needed)

1. To unclog the screen, turn off the faucets.

2. Disconnect the hose from the faucet on the wall and look inside the opening for the screen.

3. Remove the screen and clean out the junk that has collected there. Do this for both the hot- and cold-water hoses.

4. Reinsert the screen and reconnect the hose, being careful not to overtighten.

If the water still seems too slow in filling, check the other end of each hose for a similar clogging problem. When replacing the hoses, make sure you attach them to the proper faucets. Unfortunately, if all this work does not fix the problem, the pipe is probably clogged somewhere else, which will require the work of a plumber.

If no water enters the machine, detach the connecting hoses from the machine and place them in a bucket. Turn on the machine. If water comes through the hoses the problem is with the machine and you should call a service repairperson. If no water comes out, call a plumber.

Drainage Dilemmas

If the opposite problem occurs and the water does not drain out, there may be a kink in the drain hose that needs to be straightened. Sometimes suds or other objects block the drain. If this is the case, turn off the machine, bail out the suds, and remove any foreign objects. If you do not find anything blocking the drain, call a service repairperson.

Leaky Machine

If your washer leaks, the likely culprit is a loose or damaged hose.
<u>Tools to Have on Hand:</u> vise grips (as needed), straight-slot or Phillips screwdriver, pliers (as needed)

If your machine has a back panel:

1. Pull the machine away from the wall and remove the back panel.
2. Turn the machine on and watch it wash from the back. If you see any leaks, turn off and unplug the machine, shut off the water faucets and detach the water inlet hoses. Follow instructions 3, 4, and 5 below.

If the inside of your machine is accessed from the bottom:

1. Unplug your machine, shut off the water faucets, and detach the water inlet hoses.
2. Lay your washer face down on the floor so that the bottom is exposed. Remember that the machine is heavy, so ask a friend to help you.
3. Check all the hoses inside your machine.
4. If one of the internal hoses is loose, tighten the clamp with a screwdriver or by pinching it with a pair of pliers.
5. If the hose is cracked or brittle, it needs to be replaced. Sections of hose can be purchased at any hardware or plumbing supply store. Make sure the new hose you install is the same length as the old one.

Hopefully these steps will solve the problem. However, if your washing machine continues to leak, the problem is more serious and will require a professional.

Damaged Clothes

If all of a sudden your washing machine starts to damage your clothes, there is no need to start looking for a new machine. This problem can probably be fixed.

<u>Tools to Have on Hand:</u> straight-slot or Phillips screwdriver, adjustable wrench or vise grips

Check first to see if there is an object stuck in the basket (the container holding your clothes) that needs to be removed. While inspecting the basket, check for rough edges that may also be causing the problem. If this is the case, call a service person to replace the basket. The other possible cause of trouble is that your agitator is cracked and clothes are catching in it.

1. Examine your agitator for cracks. If you find any cracks, you will need to replace the agitator.

2. To remove the agitator, unscrew the plastic cap on top (some caps must be pryed off). When you remove the cap, you will see a stud that holds the agitator in place.

3. Unscrew the stud with an adjustable wrench or vise grips and lift the agitator off of its shaft.

4. Write down the make and model number of your washing machine, and purchase a new agitator from an appliance parts center. Install it by reversing these directions.

Installing a New Washing Machine

Installing a washing machine couldn't be easier, provided all the plumbing connections are in place. Most building codes require that hot- and cold-water connections and a drain pipe be installed in new housing units. If you live in an old home that doesn't have the proper connections or if you wish to move your washing machine to a new location, you will need to have a plumber install your machine. Assuming the connections are there, however, simply screw on the hot- and cold-water supply hoses, connect the drain hose, and plug in your machine. Make sure the hot connection on the machine is attached to the hose leading to the hot-water hose. Each brand of washing machine is different, so follow the installation instructions provided with your new machine.

ENERGY SAVER

Water Temperature
Wash clothes in warm or cold water, rinse with cold water. Use hot water only when absolutely necessary.

Clothes Dryer

PROBLEM	CAUSE	REMEDY	PAGE
Electric dryer not drying properly	Lint-clogged	Remove lint	67
	Venting hose kinked	Straighten hose	68
	Venting hose blocked	Remove obstruction	68
	Dryer overloaded	Remove some of load	68
	Located in cold area of house	Adjust temperature or move dryer	68
	Faulty thermostat or burned-out heating element	Call service repairperson	68
	Broken belt	Call service repairperson	68
Gas dryers not heating	Pilot light out	Light pilot light	68–69
	Faulty electronic igniter	Call service repairperson	69
	No gas	Fill gas tank	69

Save Time and Money

Learn as much as you can about what's wrong before calling for help.

How Dryers Work

An electric dryer operates with a motor, blower, timer, and heating element. As the motor rotates the drum, the blower pushes hot air heated by heating coils into the drum. This hot, dry air circulates around the clothes and then exits through the lint trap and the exhaust vent. In gas dryers, a gas burner ignited by an electronic igniter or a pilot light heats the air.

Although problems with the dryer are often beyond our capability to fix on our own, you will not be wasting time if you undertake simple investigations. It is always better in dealing with the repairperson to have an understanding of the problem. In addition, you can often get a phone estimate if you can identify the problem.

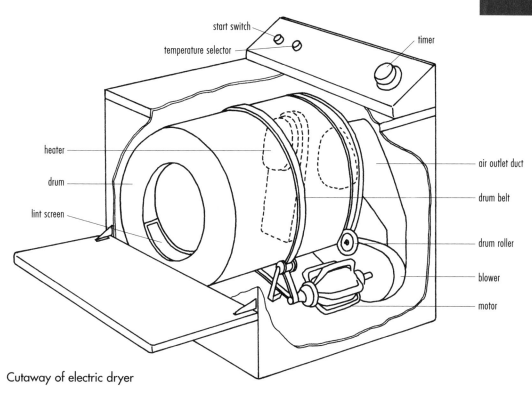

start switch

temperature selector

timer

heater

drum

lint screen

air outlet duct

drum belt

drum roller

blower

motor

Cutaway of electric dryer

Drying Problems

If your electric dryer is not drying properly, check the lint screen for a build-up of lint. Each dryer has a different method of collecting lint. Read the directions in your owner's manual for cleaning lint and clean the lint screen each time you use the dryer.

<u>Tools to Have on Hand:</u> straight-slot or Phillips screwdriver, vacuum cleaner (optional)

- If the lint is removed and the dryer still does not heat properly, check the outside venting system. Make sure that the vent hose and outlet on the outside of the house are clear of obstructions and free of lint, and that the hose is not kinked.

• Other things to consider when the dryer is taking too long to dry your clothes are whether the exhaust system is too long, the dryer is overloaded, or the dryer is located in a cold area of the house (do not operate in an area where the temperature is below 50 degrees).

• If there is no heat, check the fuse box and see if one of the two fuses has burned out. If this is the case, replace the fuse and try the dryer again. If a circuit breaker controls the circuit, call a professional. You may have a faulty thermostat or a burned-out heating element.

Repairing Gas Dryer

Depending on the type of gas dryer you have, if it is not heating, either the pilot light is out or the electronic ignition is faulty or your propane tank is empty.

<u>Tools to Have on Hand:</u> straight-slot or Phillips screwdriver

Relighting the Pilot Light. Try to find the pilot light when it is lit so you can locate it easily if it goes out. If it goes out, open the access panel located on the front of the dryer at the bottom. Light the pilot, following the instructions written down near the panel, or check your manual.

SAFETY TIP
Gas Leak
If there is strong gas odor, open the windows and leave the house. Do not touch any light or other electrical switches and call the utility company from a neighbor's house.

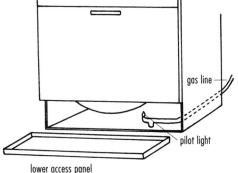

lower access panel

The gas pilot light is located behind an access panel at the bottom front of the dryer.

ENERGY SAVER
Lint-Clogged Dryer
A dryer that is clogged with lint is forced to work harder, which wastes electricity and shortens the life of your appliance. At least once a year remove the lint that has collected inside the machine.

• Unplug the electrical cord before beginning work to avoid receiving an electrical shock.
• Disconnect the exhaust vent located in the back of the machine and pull the machine out from the wall.
• Next, remove the back panel from the dryer and the lint and dust should be readily visible.
• Use a vacuum cleaner with a brush attachment or a dusting brush to clean the interior parts of your machine. Be careful not to damage anything. Reconnect the exhaust vent hose, and move the dryer back into position.

Some gas dryers with pilots have a safety device that shuts off the gas supply if the burner fails to light in a short time. To see if this is the problem, shut the dryer off. Wait a few minutes for the safety device to reset. Try to light the pilot again.

Faulty Electronic Igniter. Newer gas dryers have electronic igniters. If the igniter fails to produce a flame, call a service repairperson.

Dryer Not Rotating

A dryer is run by a belt. If the dryer is not rotating, the problem is most probably caused by a broken belt. Call a service repairperson to replace it.

Propane
If the pilot won't light and you use propane instead of natural gas, check the tank: you are probably out of gas.

ENERGY SAVER

Energy-Efficient Drying

The best way to save energy with your dryer is to shorten the drying time.

- If you have a moisture sensing control, use it, because it will automatically turn off the dryer when the clothes are dry.
- Use your dryer only when it is full. Two small loads consume far more energy than one full load.
- Keep the lint screen and the outside exhaust of your dryer clean.
- Try hanging the clothes on the line. It's fun to be outside when the weather is nice, and the clothes seem fresher and cleaner when you use a solar dryer.
- Finally, if you are considering purchasing a gas dryer, choose one with an electric ignition rather than a pilot light. An electric ignition can cut your gas usage by as much as one third.

Refrigerator Repairs

PROBLEM	CAUSE	REMEDY	PAGE
Not cool enough		Adjust temperature	70
	Dusty condenser coils	Clean condenser coils	71
	Cracked or brittle door gasket	Replace door gasket	72
	Faulty defrost mechanism	Replace defrost mechanism	72
Smelly	Spoiled food	Clean refrigerator and lower temperature	73
	Dirty drain pad	Clean drain pad	73
Light not working	Burned out bulb	Replace bulb	73

While you may not be able to fix all the things that go wrong with a refrigerator, taking simple preventive maintenance steps will extend the life of your appliance and help it to run more efficiently.

Adjusting the Temperature

If you suspect that your refrigerator or freezer is not cool enough, take its temperature.

<u>Tool to Have on Hand:</u> outdoor thermometer

Place an outdoor thermometer in both the freezer and the middle of the refrigerator compartments for a few minutes each. The temperature in the freezer should range from 0° to 8°F and in the refrigerator, from 38° to 42°F. Higher temperatures may cause food to spoil while lower temperatures waste energy. Adjust the temperature on the panel in the refrigerator (the higher the number, the colder the temperature) and check the temperature with a thermometer a few hours later.

ENERGY SAVER
Maintaining Your Refrigerator
By cleaning the condenser coils periodically and by making sure your gasket seal is tight, you will extend the life of your appliance and reduce its energy use.

Cleaning the Condenser Coils

If adjusting the temperature doesn't work, clean the dust and lint from the condenser coils, which are either on the back of or underneath your refrigerator. Dust insulates the coils, making it difficult for them to work efficiently.

<u>Tools to Have on Hand:</u> vacuum cleaner (optional), bottle brush (optional), straight-slot or Phillips screwdriver

1. Unplug the appliance and pull it away from the wall. The coils cover about three fourths of the back of your refrigerator and look like a grill.

2. Clean the coils using the brush attachment on your vacuum cleaner.

3. To get to the coils under your refrigerator, remove the grill panel that sits about half an inch above the floor. This panel is held in place by snaps or small screws that are easily detached.

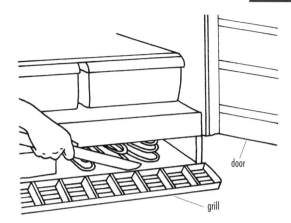

door

grill

Use vacuum attachments to clean coils.

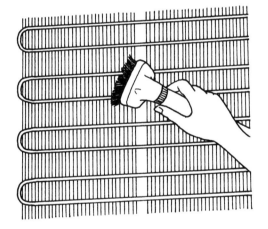

Condenser coils may be located on the back or underneath your refrigerator.

4. Once the panel is removed, remove the dust and lint on the coils with your vacuum cleaner brush or a long-handled bottle brush.

5. Before reattaching the grill, empty the water from the drain pan located under the coils. Water collects in the pan when your refrigerator defrosts. This pan is large and cumbersome, so be careful not to spill the water.

6. Replace the pan and the grill panel.

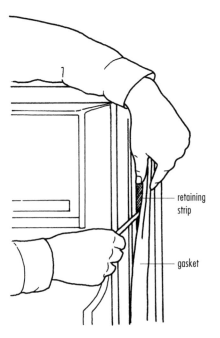

Working on one side at a time, remove a section of the old gasket and align the new one in its place.

Replacing the Door Gasket

Door gaskets leak cold air when they have cracks or become brittle. You may be able to feel the leak by running your hand along the door's edge. Another way to check the gasket is to close the door on a piece of paper and then pull the paper out. As you pull out the paper you should feel tension. If you don't, then the gasket needs to be replaced.

Replacing the gasket is not a difficult job, but you should call the parts supply store to see if they have a replacement gasket for your refrigerator model before taking it out. They may have to order one for you. Before securing the new gasket in place, make sure the refrigerator door is aligned properly.

<u>Tools to Have on Hand:</u> straight-slot or Phillips screwdriver

1. Once you have a new gasket on hand, soak it in warm water to soften it and make it easier to work with.

2. Unplug the refrigerator. This is both a safety precaution and a way to save energy while you work.

3. Replace one side of the gasket at a time. Pull back the old gasket and you will see the retaining strip and screws. Take out the screws on the top edge of the door and the ones along the side.

4. Remove the top section of the gasket and align a new section in its place. Insert the retaining strip and replace the screws, leaving them loose.

5. Repeat these directions to install the remaining three sides. Align the door properly and then tighten all the screws holding the gasket in place.

Replacing Defrost Mechanism

It is also possible that your defrost mechanism is defective. When the defrost cycle does not come on, the coils ice up, which inhibits cooling. The problem is either with the defrost timer or heater. Replacing these parts is not an easy task and should be left to a professional.

There are other possible reasons for a refrigerator not cooling properly. If you have not been able to solve your problem, call a professional.

Saving Energy in Your Refrigerator

- Refrigerators that are defrosted manually use less electricity than those that defrost automatically.
- Make sure the seals on your refrigerator door are airtight.
- Many refrigerators have an "energy-saver" switch (check the manual if you don't see it). Leave it in the "normal" position unless condensation on the outside of your refrigerator is a significant problem. Leaving the switch on continually can increase electricity usage by 10 to 20%.

Fixing a Smelly Refrigerator

If your refrigerator begins to smell, it is possible that food is spoiling.
<u>Tool to Have on Hand:</u> outdoor thermometer

    1. Throw out the bad food and wash the inside of the refrigerator with a solution of baking soda and warm water.

    2. Check the temperature of the refrigerator with a thermometer. It should be between 38° and 42°F.

    3. It is also possible that the drain pan underneath the refrigerator is dirty. Empty the water and clean the pan with a mild detergent and warm water.

    4. If all of the above are in good order, it may be that your breaker strips are damaged, which is enabling moisture to enter the insulation between the inner and outer walls of your refrigerator. This problem causes odor and also reduces the cooling efficiency of your refrigerator. To solve this problem, you will need to call for professional help.

Replacing Light Bulb in Refrigerator

When the light in your refrigerator burns out, it is very easy to replace. Find the bulb, unscrew it, and take it to a hardware store to find an exact replacement. Screw in the new appliance bulb, and you are all set.

Icemaker

PROBLEM	CAUSE	REMEDY	PAGE
Not making ice		Reset	75
	Water supply line frozen	Thaw water supply line	75
		Call service repairperson	75

Installing an Icemaker

Many refrigerators are purchased with the icemaker already installed. If you have a refrigerator with an icemaker already in it, to hook it up you need to attach it to a cold-water source.

<u>Tools to Have on Hand:</u> icemaker installation kit, pipe tapper, electric drill (as needed)

Installation requires a hose to be inserted into a cold-water pipe, which is often located in the basement. The best way to accomplish this task is to purchase an icemaker installation kit at any hardware or plumbing supply store. It consists of plastic tubing (make sure you purchase enough to run from the refrigerator to the nearest cold-water pipe) and a pipe tapper. If the refrigerator is on the first floor and the water pipe is in the basement or under the house, you will need to drill a hole into the basement or through to the outside. If your cold-water hose connects to an outside water pipe, make sure to insulate it so that it doesn't freeze. This task will require an electric drill with a bit that is at least the size of the plastic tubing.

1. Shut off the water in the house as described on pages 8–9.

2. The next step is to get cold water from a pipe into your refrigerator. Attach the plastic tubing to the icemaker valve at the back of the refrigerator.

3. If the cold-water pipe is in the basement or under the house, drill a hole into the basement or through to the outside.

4.   Insert the plastic tubing through the hole and direct it toward the nearest cold-water pipe (test to make sure that you are choosing a cold-water pipe by feeling it).

5.   Now follow the directions on the pipe tapper package for tapping into the pipe. Put the tapping device onto the pipe. This device has its own needle to tap into the pipe. Once this needle is inserted, it is self-sealing so that it should not leak. Now attach the plastic tubing to the valve on the pipe tapper, turn the water back on, and the job is completed.

Repairing an Icemaker

Sometimes your icemaker will stop making ice for no apparent reason. Very often all that is required is to reset it if your machine has a reset button. Also the arm on the side of the machine might be stuck in the up position which turns the icemaker off. If it is, pull the arm down. Also remove any stuck ice cubes. Another possible reason that an icemaker will not make ice is because the water supply line is frozen. To check this:

1.   Reach into the icemaker and feel the tray where the ice is formed. If there is no water or ice in this tray, you know that the water is not entering the unit.

2.   In this case, you must defrost the freezer to thaw the line.

3.   Now turn the icemaker back on and it should work.

4.   If it doesn't, it is a good idea to have the entire unit serviced.

Pipe tapper

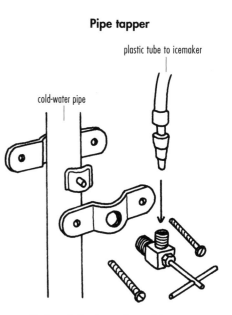

plastic tube to icemaker

cold-water pipe

To install the icemaker tubing, use a pipe tapper to tap into the cold-water pipe.

Electric Range

PROBLEM	CAUSE	REMEDY	PAGE
Damaged wire		Repair wire	76
Faulty burner		Replace burner	76
All burners not working	Circuit breaker off or fuse blown	Turn on circuit breaker or replace burned-out fuse	76
Faulty heating element in oven		Replace heating element	77
Light burned out in oven		Replace bulb	77

Replacing Burner on Electric Stove

An electric range operates on two circuits and the electricity is controlled by switches, a timer, and a thermostat. When a burner on the top of the stove stops working, it can be replaced without much difficulty. First check to see if the other burners are working. If none of the burners on your stove works, the circuit breaker has probably flipped off or the fuse has blown.

Tools to Have on Hand: straight-slot or Phillips screwdriver (as needed)

1. Check the circuit breaker or fuse box in the basement to see if any breakers are turned off or fuses have blown. If you find a circuit breaker off, flip it back on. If a fuse has blown, replace it with a fuse of the same amperage.

2. If the other burners work, turn off the power to the range at the circuit breaker box and then lift the bad burner up.

3. Next, remove the chrome ring from around the burner.

4. There are two different ways that burners are attached to the stove. One element type simply unplugs from the stove. The other type screws into the stove. Unscrew the small screw, slip the burner out, and repair any burned or broken wires following instructions on page 54. If the wires are not the problem, disconnect them. Diagram the wire scheme and mark each wire.

5. Take the element to an appliance parts store to be replaced.

Maintaining the Hood and Filter

Above the stove, a hood collects the grease and directs odors out of the kitchen. The filter under the hood should be kept clean so the fan can do its job properly.

Tools to Have on Hand: straight-slot screwdriver (as needed)

To clean the filter, gently pry it off and clean it with soap and hot water (see drawing at right). If it becomes caked with grease and too dirty to clean, the filter can also be replaced for little cost.

Replacing Heating Element in Electric Oven

There is nothing worse when baking a cake than to find that one of the heating elements in the oven is not working. You end up with a half-burned, half-cooked cake. It is not difficult to replace the bad element, though it may seem a little scary.

Tools to Have on Hand: straight-slot or Phillips screwdriver

1. Turn on the oven, open the door and see which element is not heating up.

2. Once this is determined, turn the oven off and remove all racks from the oven. Let the elements cool off.

3. Since the oven plug is probably inaccessible, flip the circuit breaker for the oven to *off,* or remove the appropriate fuse.

4. Next, unfasten the two screws that attach the element to the back of the oven. Also disconnect the wires that attach to the element (see drawing at right). Remember to make a diagram and mark each wire with tape so that each can be put back in its proper place.

5. Now take the element to the hardware store for replacement.

6. To put the new element back into the oven, simply reverse these directions.

Replacing the Oven Light Bulb

The light in an electric oven occasionally burns out. To replace it, unfasten the bulb and take it to the hardware store so that you are sure to purchase the right appliance bulb.

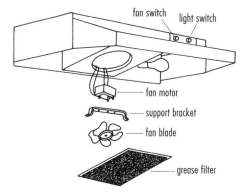

Keep filter of range hood clean.

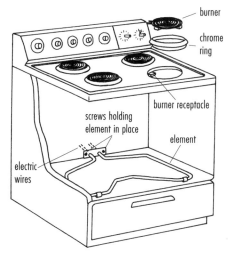

Both surface and oven heating elements are usually easy to replace. Turn off the power to the appliance before beginning the repair.

Gas Range

PROBLEM	CAUSE	REMEDY	PAGE
Burner won't light	Burner pilot light out	Light burner pilot light	79
	Burner pilot light clogged	Clean burner pilot light	79
All burners won't light	Oven pilot light out	Light oven pilot light	78–79
	Oven pilot light clogged	Clean oven pilot light	79

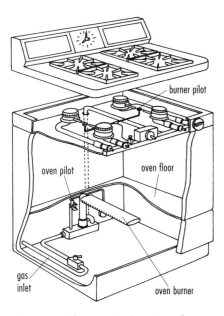

Cutaway of gas unit, showing pilot lights for surface and oven burners.

Fixing Burner in Gas Stove

Gas ranges are less complicated and generally easier to repair. In older model gas stoves, all burners are lit by a pilot light. In newer models, electronic igniters light the stove burners, and igniters or electrically heated glow bars light the oven burners. To operate efficiently, the burners must be clog-free and the flame must contain the right proportion of gas and air. When a burner won't light, there is a good chance that the pilot light is out. There is a main pilot light for the oven and usually a separate one for each burner. If none of the burners light, the main pilot is probably out. If only one burner is not working, then the burner pilot is out. If relighting the appropriate pilot does not solve the problem and you use propane, check your gas tank and you may discover that it needs to be refilled. In newer model gas stoves the electronic igniter, switch, or module may be faulty. Call a professional to fix this.

Relighting Main Pilot Light

The pilot light for the oven is usually located underneath the oven floor, which can be removed. If there is a slight gas smell from the pilot not being lit, open the oven door to dissipate it. If there is a strong gas odor, open the windows, shut off the main gas valve (see page 92), do not touch any electrical switches, and call the utility company.

Tools to Have on Hand: straight-slot screwdriver or butter knife

1. Make sure the gas is turned off on the oven and stove. Open the oven door and remove the oven racks. Locate the floor of the oven, pry it up, and take it out.

2. You will then see the pilot light, which can be reignited with a match. Your oven should automatically turn on now.

Relighting Burner Pilot Lights

To relight pilot lights for the burners, take the top of the stove off. Though this may sound difficult, it is actually quite simple.

<u>Tools to Have on Hand:</u> straight-slot screwdriver or butter knife

1. Remove anything from the top of the range that will fall off when raised.

2. Lift off the stove top. Once the top is removed, the 2 or 4 pilot lights will be visible, depending on the type of stove.

3. Relight each one that does not have a small flame.

4. If you use propane instead of natural gas, check to see if your gas tank needs to be refilled.

Cleaning the Burner Pilot Lights

A gas pilot light that is clogged with food, grease, or dust won't light or stay lit. Cleaning the pilot light is an easy task.

<u>Tool to Have on Hand:</u> wooden toothpick

If your pilot light has a protective metal shield, remove it by pressing in the tabs on either side. Then simply insert a wooden toothpick into the pilot hole and gently move it up and down, being careful not to enlarge the pilot light hole (see drawing at right). Clean each of the burner pilots this same way.

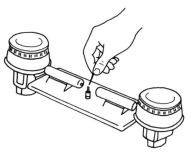

Gently draw a wooden toothpick up and down in the pilot hole to clean it.

Cleaning the Oven Pilot Light

A gas oven burner that is clogged produces an uneven flame. That leads to poor baking results and/or a gas odor when the oven is turned on. You can smell the problem.

<u>Tool to Have on Hand:</u> sewing needle

To unclog the burner, turn off the oven and insert a sewing needle into each hole along the sides of the burner. Now test the burner again. The problem should be solved.

Repairing the Dishwasher

PROBLEM	CAUSE	REMEDY	PAGE
Dishes not getting clean	Water not hot enough	Raise temperature of water heater; call professional to replace heating element	81
	Strainer is clogged	Clean strainer	82
	Defective detergent dispenser	Replace any broken parts	82
	Spray arm not working properly	Remove obstacles blocking movement of spray tower; replace spray tower	83
	Spray arm clogged	Unclog spray arm	83
Dishwasher noisy and vibrates	Not on solid flooring	Put on solid flooring	84
	Height of legs uneven	Adjust leg height	84
Dishwasher not running, cleaning, filling, draining, drying	Drain blocked	Unblock drain	84
Water overflowing from dishwasher	Tank cracked	Seal with water sealant	84
	Hose is split	Install new hose	84
Leaky dishwasher	Hose clamp loose	Tighten clamp	84–85

Although dishwashers are complex machines, many of their problems are quite easy to fix. If your dishes are not getting clean, follow the procedures discussed below.

Adjusting the Water Temperature

The first thing to check is the water temperature.

<u>Tool to Have on Hand:</u> meat thermometer

Most dishwashers require a water temperature of 140°F or more to function effectively. A lower temperature won't dissolve grease or remove hardened food. To be sure that the water is hot enough, run the hot-water kitchen tap to the right temperature before turning on the dishwasher. Check your owner's manual to see if your machine has a booster heater.

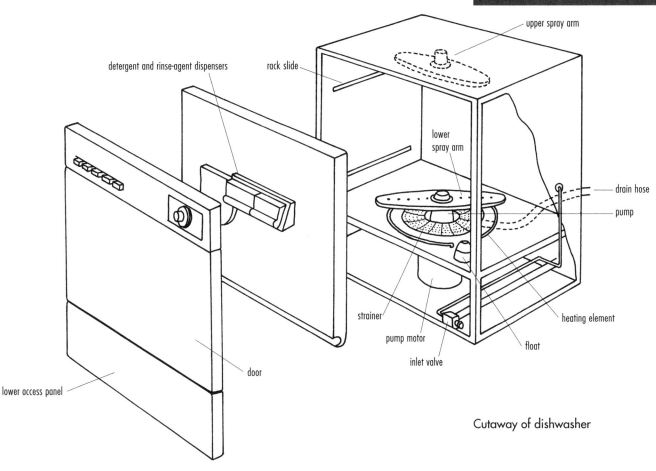

upper spray arm

detergent and rinse-agent dispensers

rack slide

lower spray arm

drain hose

pump

strainer

pump motor

inlet valve

float

heating element

door

lower access panel

Cutaway of dishwasher

A booster heater enables you to keep your water heater at a lower setting (110° to 120°F), which conserves energy.

1. You can test the water temperature by turning on your dishwasher and then opening the door during the first wash cycle.

2. Place a meat thermometer or candy thermometer in the hot water at the bottom of the tub. If the temperature is below 140°F, you will need to raise the temperature of your water heater or replace the heating element. Unfortunately, replacing the element is a difficult job and will require a professional.

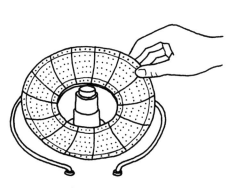

Remove the strainer located under the dish rack and rinse or clean out obstacles.

Unclogging the Strainer

The strainer is located inside the dishwasher below the tray that holds plates and underneath the heating element. Occasionally it becomes clogged, affecting the cleaning action.

<u>Tools to Have on Hand:</u> straight-slot or Phillips screwdriver

1. Turn off the power to your machine at the circuit breaker box.

2. Remove the dish rack and unfasten the screws holding the strainer in place. In some models, the strainer is not accessible, and in others, the spray arm must be removed to reach the strainer.

3. Clean out any obstacle or gunk and replace the strainer.

Adjusting the Detergent Dispenser

If that doesn't solve the problem, the detergent dispenser may not be releasing detergent. To check, you will have to remove the door panel.

<u>Tools to Have on Hand:</u> straight-slot or Phillips screwdriver

1. Begin by turning off the electrical power to the dishwasher at the circuit breaker box.

2. Open the door and unfasten the screws that are located along the edge of the door. Once these screws are removed, the panel will slide off from the door and the detergent dispenser mechanism will be readily apparent (see drawing on page 81).

3. Move the arm of the mechanism back and forth by hand to make sure that it doesn't stick. You should also compare the mechanism with the diagram in your owner's manual to check for broken parts. Replace any broken parts and refasten the door panel.

ENERGY SAVER

Saving Energy in the Dishwasher

It may surprise you to learn that an efficient dishwasher consumes less energy than washing dishes by hand. Here are some ways to save even more.

- Do not waste hot water pre-rinsing dishes. Many newer dishwashers require only that the food be scraped off.
- Fill the dishwasher completely before using it.
- Allow your dishes to air dry, which can save up to 10% of the total energy consumed.

Freeing the Spray Arm

The spray arm could also be the culprit. The spray arm is located at the bottom of your dishwasher, just above the motor (see drawing at right). It usually comes with a telescoping spray tower.

<u>Tools to Have on Hand:</u> straight-slot or Phillips screwdriver (as needed)

1. Turn off the power to the appliance at the circuit breaker box.
2. Remove the dish rack.
3. Check first to see that the spray tower moves up and down and spins freely.
4. If it does not, unscrew the tower and see if you can discover what is blocking the movement. If you cannot correct this problem, you will need to replace the spray tower.

Cleaning the Spray Arm

The spray arm may also be clogged.

<u>Tools to Have on Hand:</u> straight-slot or Phillips screwdriver, toothpick or thin wire

1. Once you have unscrewed the spray tower, lift off the spray arm by unfastening the screw that holds it in place.
2. With a toothpick or wire, unclog the holes on both sides of the spray arm.
3. Shake and rinse the spray arm with water and reassemble the parts. That should solve the problem and hopefully your dishwasher will now produce clean dishes.

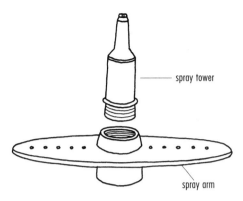

spray tower

spray arm

The spray tower should move up and down and spin freely.

If your dishwasher has a top spray arm, fix or clean it as described above.

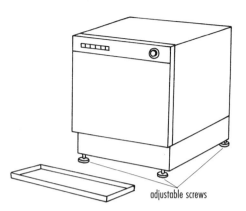

To level the appliance, remove the bottom front panel to access the adjustable screws on the legs.

Balancing the Dishwasher

Dishwashers that are noisy and vibrate excessively are probably not on solid flooring, or the height of the legs of the dishwasher may be uneven.

<u>Tools to Have on Hand:</u> straight-slot or Phillips screwdriver

You can adjust the front legs by removing the bottom front panel with a screwdriver. The legs screw in and out to raise and lower the machine (see drawing at left).

Repairing an Overflowing Dishwasher

1. Turn off the water supply and the power to the dishwasher at the circuit breaker.

2. Open the door and check the drain cover on the bottom of the machine. There may be something blocking it.

3. Remove the obstacle and try the dishwasher again.

Repairing Leak Caused by a Crack

If the dishwasher is leaking from the bottom, first make sure that you are not using too much soap and that the dishwasher is loaded properly. It is also possible that the tank is cracked.

<u>Tools to Have on Hand:</u> straight-slot or Phillips screwdriver, pliers

1. Before beginning your work, make sure to turn off power to your machine at the circuit breaker or fuse box.

2. If you discover a crack in the tank, seal it with a silicone rubber sealant.

Repairing Leak Caused by Faulty Hose

It is also possible that a hose is split or that a hose clamp has become loose. To check for this possibility, you will have to remove the lower front panel that sits between the floor and your dishwasher's door.

1. With the power turned off to the machine, remove any retaining screws and pull the panel down or lift it off from its hooks.

2. Examine the hoses for cracks or splits and make sure that the clamps are securely fastened. If a clamp is loose, you will need to reposition it.

3. Take a pair of pliers and squeeze the spring clamp, which will enable you to move it in a way that tightens it.

4. To disconnect a damaged hose, move the clamps toward the middle of the hose and pull both ends of the hose out. Have a shallow pan ready to catch any water that escapes when the hose is removed. Bring the old hose to the hardware store to replace it, reconnect the new hose at both ends, and move the clamps into position to secure it.

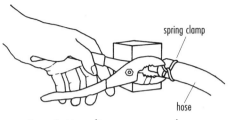

spring clamp

hose

Step 3: Use pliers to remove the spring clamp that holds the hose in place.

Garbage Disposal

PROBLEM	CAUSE	REMEDY	PAGE
Will not run	Jammed with object	Turn off circuit breaker to disposal and remove object	85

When your garbage disposal will not run, there is a good chance that it is jammed with a small bone, a kitchen utensil, or heavy fruit rinds.

<u>Tools to Have on Hand:</u> broom handle, kitchen tongs or pliers

1. If the disposal is not making noise when you try to run it, first press the reset button under the sink on the disposal motor.

2. Before working on the disposal, turn off the power to the unit at the circuit breaker.

3. If you suspect there is a jam, insert a broom handle into the unit until it comes into contact with the flywheel at the base of the unit. Turn the flywheel counterclockwise a few times to free the jammed object.

4. Now you should be able to remove the object with kitchen tongs or pliers. If the object is too small to reach, it will probably be ground up when the disposal is turned on.

5. Turn the power back on.

6. You will find a reset button located under the sink on the disposal motor. Push this button before trying to restart your unit. Now run the disposal to see if the problem is solved.

SAFETY TIP

Caution with the Garbage Disposal
Always turn off the power to the disposal at the circuit breaker before trying to fix it. Never stick your fingers into the disposal!

How to Keep Disposal Running Smoothly

- Do not pour grease down the drain and into the disposal. If the disposal is running sluggishly, try pouring boiling water into the unit to dissolve any accumulated grease.
- Never use chemical drain cleaners to remove a clog in your disposal. These chemicals can damage the plastic and rubber parts in your appliance.
- Check your owner's manual to determine what can and cannot go into the disposal. Never try to grind up hard objects such as lobster claws unless your owner's manual says that the disposal will accept them. Such objects can make the motor overheat, which will trip the overload protector. Do not put anything fibrous, like banana peels, into the disposal.
- Insert garbage loosely. If you pack in too much at once, you can jam the disposal.
- Never insert inorganic waste such as metal, plastic, or rubber objects into your disposal. Such objects can seriously damage your appliance as well as the plumbing.
- When operating your disposal, keep a steady stream of cold water running. This assists the shredding process and also helps to congeal grease so that it breaks up and washes down the drain. Allow the water to run for a minute or so after turning off the disposal so that the garbage is flushed down the drain.
- An excellent way to deodorize your disposal is to grind lemon or orange peels.
- The best way to keep the drain free is to dispose of garbage promptly and not allow it to sit there overnight.
- Place a cover over the disposal when it is not in use. This will prevent objects such as silverware from falling in it and causing the disposal to jam.

Vacuum Cleaner

PROBLEM	CAUSE	REMEDY	PAGE
Decreased suction	Bag is full	Change bag	87
	Hose blocked	Unblock hose	87
Brush beater doesn't turn	Drive belt stretched or broken	Insert new belt	87

Decreased Suction

A decline in your machine's suction is usually caused by a full dust bag. Simply empty or replace the bag. A blocked hose may also be the cause. Pins, paper clips, nails, and screws get caught crosswise in your hose, which creates the blockage.

Tool to Have on Hand: broom handle (as needed)

1. Disconnect the hose, turn on the power, and place your hand over the air intake. If you feel strong suction, the hose is blocked.

2. With the hose disconnected, you can remove the blockage by shaking the hose or by carefully inserting a broom handle into it.

Brush Problems

If the brush beater no longer turns, it is almost certain that your drive belt has either stretched or is broken.

Tools to Have on Hand: straight-slot or Phillips screwdriver (as needed)

1. Make sure your machine is unplugged.

2. Turn your vacuum cleaner upside down and remove the belt cover plate. If the belt is broken, your owner's manual should show you how it is attached.

3. Assuming the belt is still intact, lift it from the motor shaft pulley, remove the brush beater, and the other end of the belt will slide off.

4. To insert a new belt, place it in the middle of the brush beater, and reattach the brush beater. Then stretch the belt and place it around the motor shaft pulley.

5. Replace the cover plate, plug in your machine, and test the results of your work.

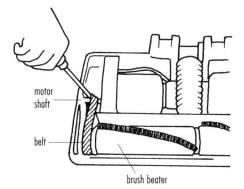

motor shaft

belt

brush beater

Use pliers to remove the belt from the motor shaft pulley.

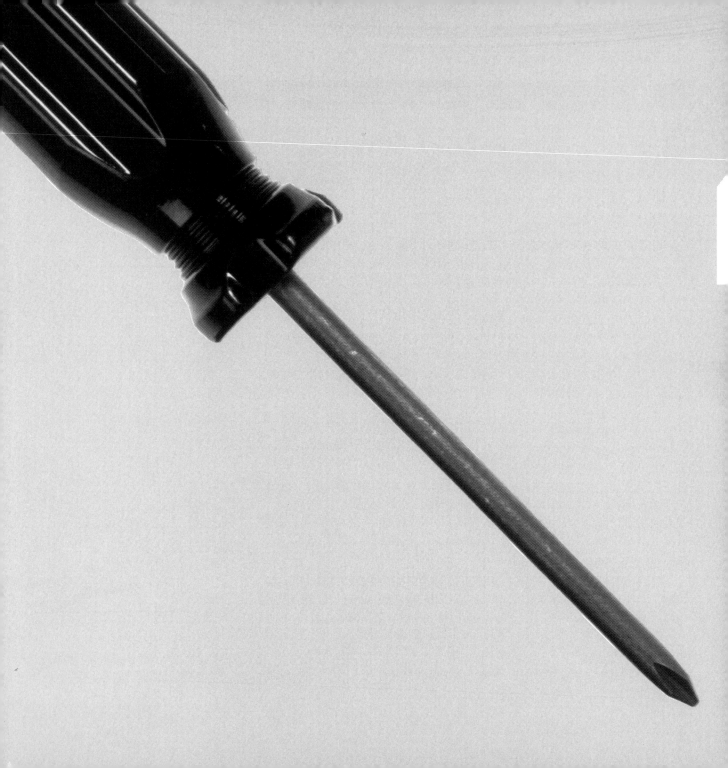

Chapter Four

Heating and Cooling

Heating and Cooling

AT A GLANCE

- furnaces
- air conditioners
- wood stoves
- caulking and weatherstripping
- insulation

and more

Central Heating Systems

Many homes have forced-air heating systems in which a gas or oil furnace heats air and distributes it through ducts throughout the house. Other systems use hot water or steam as the source of heat. In hot-water systems, water is heated in a boiler and carried through pipes to radiators, baseboard pipes, or coils in the floor. Steam-heating systems distribute steam from the boiler to radiators. A third way to heat is with electricity. Either electricity passes through heating elements to produce heat or an electric heat pump brings in outside air and heats it.

Oil and Gas Furnaces

PROBLEM	CAUSE	REMEDY	PAGE
Oil furnace not working	Emergency switch off	Turn on emergency switch	91
		Call utility company	
	Circuit breaker off or fuse blown	Turn on circuit breaker or replace blown fuse	91
		Call utility company	
	Oil tank empty, gauge stuck	Check tank	91
	Timer not set correctly	Check timer	91
	Dirty or corroded contact points	Clean off contact points	91
Gas furnace not working	Pilot light out	Relight pilot; call utility company	91
No heat in one or two rooms	Duct joints unsealed	Seal duct joints	95
	Heating system unbalanced	Open heating vents in cold rooms and close vents in warm rooms	95
		Call professional	

If you wake up in the morning to a cold house, it is likely that the furnace has shut off or is not operating properly. The best thing to do is to call the utility company. Many furnaces are difficult and dangerous to fix. The utility company will most likely respond quickly to your call. There are a few things, however, that you can do before calling the utility company.

Diagnosing a Faulty Oil Furnace

If your oil furnace doesn't come on, you can test several things before getting involved in real repairs.

<u>Tools to Have on Hand:</u> straight-slot or Phillips screwdriver (as needed)

1. First, make sure that the emergency switch is turned on. This switch is usually found close to the furnace or in the basement stairway. It is often painted red and looks like a regular light switch. This switch functions like a circuit breaker and is a safety device. If it flips off again, call the utility company.

2. Next, check the fuse box or circuit breaker. Replace the blown fuse or reset the circuit breaker if that is the problem. Call the utility company if the new fuse blows or the circuit breaker trips again.

3. Move the thermostat up a few degrees. This should trigger the furnace to turn on.

4. Check the gauge on the oil tank. It is possible that the gauge has become stuck on full when your tank is actually empty.

5. You should also determine if the furnace has a thermostat with a day and night setting. Remove the thermostat covering and check to see if a power outage has caused the timer to operate off-cycle.

6. Finally, turn off the power to the furnace at the circuit breaker box and with the cover off, find the contact points. If there is dirt or corrosion on the points, the furnace will not come on. Clean off these points by passing a piece of paper between them.

Diagnosing a Faulty Gas Furnace

For furnaces that use natural gas for fuel, a common problem is a pilot light that has gone out. This problem can usually be easily remedied, but you must know what you are doing.

<u>Tools to Have on Hand:</u> pliers (as needed), wire brush (as needed)

My first advice is to ask the utility company to send someone to show you how to do it. Remember you are literally "playing with fire," and thus it is important to be very cautious. For those of you who would like to do it yourself, there is usually a plate attached to the furnace with directions on it (see drawing below). Follow these directions, but make sure to turn off the valve that controls the gas supply into the furnace.

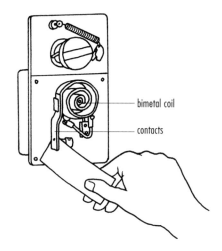

bimetal coil

contacts

Step 6: Clean thermostat contact points by passing a piece of paper between them.

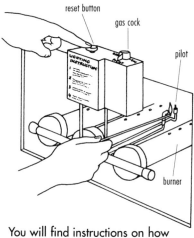

reset button

gas cock

pilot

burner

You will find instructions on how to relight the pilot on your gas furnace.

Many new gas furnaces have an electronic ignition system instead of a pilot light. These systems tend to get fouled up with carbon deposits on the burner. This will prevent proper ignition. It is a good idea to clean your furnace burners with a wire brush each fall. Check your furnace manual for instructions.

Turn Off the Gas

There is a main shut-off valve near the meter that controls the flow of gas into your house (see drawing below) and individual shut-off valves located at the back of each appliance that operates with gas. All of these shut-off valves operate in the same way. The valve is open when the handle is parallel to the supply pipe and closed when the handle is perpendicular to the supply pipe. If you have problems moving the handle, try using pliers or a wrench. Follow the instructions and make sure to turn off the valve that controls the gas supply to the furnace.

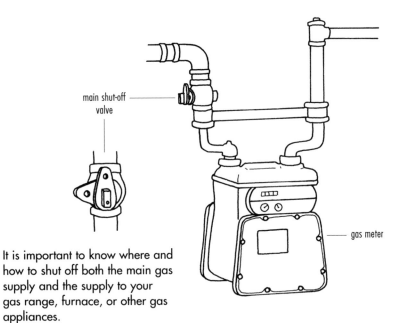

main shut-off valve

gas meter

It is important to know where and how to shut off both the main gas supply and the supply to your gas range, furnace, or other gas appliances.

Electric Furnaces and Heat Pumps

PROBLEM	CAUSE	REMEDY	PAGE
Electric furnace not working	Thermostat off or low	Adjust thermostat	94
	Circuit breaker off or fuse blown	Turn on circuit breaker or replace blown fuse	94
	Filter dirty	Replace filter or defective blower	94–95
	Burned-out heating element	Call repairperson	
Heat pump not working	Thermostat off or low	Adjust thermostat	94
	Circuit breaker off or fuse blown	Turn on circuit breaker or replace blown fuse	94
Heat pump defrost cycle not running or runs continuously	Coils covered with debris	Clean coils; call repairperson	94

Diagnosing a Faulty Electric Furnace

An electric furnace operates much like a toaster. Electric current heats resistance coils. A blower pushes air through the coils, which heats it. The hot air then moves through a duct system to specific rooms in your house. The good news is that because there are no moving parts, there is little maintenance required. Unfortunately, electric heat is the most expensive type of heat.

If your house becomes cold, first check the thermostat and make sure that a fuse has not blown or the breaker tripped. If the furnace cycles on and off frequently, it is likely that the filter needs to be replaced. For other problems, you will need to call a professional repairperson.

Diagnosing a Faulty Heat Pump

A final source of heat is the heat pump. It pumps heat out of the house in the summer and into the house in the winter.

Although electricity powers the pump, outdoor air or groundwater is the heat source — not electricity. Even cold air or water contains heat. Because the system is able to pump far more heat from the air or water than the energy the pump consumes, it is an efficient way to heat your home. The system works well until the temperature dips below 10°F, in which case backup heat is necessary.

• Heat pumps have problems similar to other furnaces when power doesn't get to the pump or the thermostat is set too low. Adjust the thermostat and check the breaker or fuse box.

• A more important problem occurs when the defrost cycle does not run or if it runs continuously. This causes the backup system to take over. The most likely cause of this problem is a heavy accumulation of ice or debris on the outdoor coil. Clean the coil, and the system should return to normal. If the ice persists, try changing the thermostat to cool. If the ice does not melt within an hour, switch to your alternate system and call a repairperson.

• Change the filter regularly. Your owner's manual provides instructions for this task.

Adjusting Heating Vents

If one of your rooms is cold and you have a forced-air system, check to make sure that the heating vents are open. They are louvered, and can be opened or closed to regulate the amount of heat you allow into the room. <u>Tools to Have on Hand:</u> straight-slot screwdriver (as needed)

To open the vent, it sometimes helps to use a screwdriver to push the metal wheel that moves the metal slats to open. It is also advisable to vacuum dirt and dust out of the vent to keep down dust in the air.

Balancing the Heat

If your furnace comes on and one or two rooms remain chilly, it may be that your forced-air heating system is out of balance.

<u>Tools to Have on Hand:</u> straight-slot screwdriver, duct tape (as needed)

1. Check to see that all the joints in the duct work are sealed with duct tape. Retape any suspicious joints.

2. Balance the heating system by closing the vents a little in the warmest rooms and opening up vents in the coldest rooms.

3. If that doesn't work, call a professional to check your furnace. Explain the problem and ask for suggestions.

4. One further possibility is to install a booster fan in the duct work in order to force the heat to out-of-the-way places. This is a difficult job and will require a professional.

ENERGY SAVER

Winter Heating Tips

- When the heat is on, keep your thermostat as low as possible. The human body gives off heat, so warm clothing provides an excellent source of insulation. Lower the thermostat to 55°F (13°C) at night. Even lowering your thermostat a few degrees will lead to considerable savings.
- Keep windows next to the thermostat tightly closed so that the rest of the house is not several degrees warmer than the area around the thermostat.
- Make sure your heating system is operating efficiently. If you have a furnace or heat pump, check the filter at least every other month during the winter. Clean the filter as needed and replace it when it appears to be worn out. Have a professional tune an oil-fired system once a year. Gas-fired systems and heat pumps need only be tuned once every two years.
- If you use an electric furnace for heating, consider a heat pump. These pumps are expensive, but they can reduce your total use of electricity for both heating and cooling by 30 to 40 percent.
- Close off unoccupied rooms or rooms not currently in use. This means shutting the heat or air conditioning vents unless you have a heat pump. Shutting vents in this case could harm the heat pump.
- Keep your fireplace damper closed when not in use. It also helps to install a glass front to keep warm air from going up the chimney.

Fireplace and Wood Stove

PROBLEM	CAUSE	REMEDY	PAGE
Smoke in house	Flue closed; leaky flue	Open flue; have flue checked by chimney sweep	96
Heat loss	Flue open with no fire	Close flue	96
	Loose mortar around damper	Remove mortar for tight damper seal	97
Inside of chimney lined with black, flaky residue	Creosote buildup	Have flue checked by chimney sweep	97

There is nothing that adds more atmosphere to a room than a warm fire in the fireplace. Before starting the fire, there are a few things to note about fireplaces.

<u>Tool to Have on Hand:</u> flashlight

First, you must make sure the chimney flue is open so that the smoke rises up the chimney and not into your room. Get a flashlight, stick your head into the fireplace, and shine the light up the chimney. It should be immediately apparent if the damper is shut. To open it, simply pull the lever that attaches to the damper.

If you found the damper shut, it was for a good reason. Heat escapes through an open flue and proceeds up your chimney. To conserve energy during the winter, keep the damper closed unless you plan to have a fire. You can also install a glass screen across the fireplace opening. By covering the fireplace opening when it is not in use, you will prevent heat loss.

Lighting the Fire

Once you are satisfied with the condition of the chimney, lighting a fire is quite easy. It is a good idea to keep the ashes left in the fireplace banked to the rear and sides. Before starting a fire, make sure that you have plenty of newspaper, some small twigs, and dry wood. Light the paper, and as the small twigs catch fire, slowly add larger pieces of wood. When adding these larger pieces of wood, be sure to space them wide enough apart so that the fire gets plenty of oxygen. This is especially important at the beginning. Wood that is lumped too close together will choke off the oxygen (smother the fire) and cause the fire to go out.

Leaky Flue

If you smell smoke fumes inside your home or if you see smoke seeping through cracks in your chimney, have your flue checked immediately. A chimney flue that leaks is dangerous. It can cause a house fire as well as bring toxic fumes into your home. This problem most often occurs in older homes. Modern chimney flues are lined with flue tiles or firebricks, which protect the flue from leaking. If you live in an older home, do not start reusing an old fireplace without having the flue checked by a registered chimney sweep.

Energy-Efficient Damper

In order to prevent heat loss in the winter, it is important that a fireplace damper have a tight seal. A common problem that prevents a damper from closing tightly is loose mortar that has collected around the edges. Remove the mortar bits with your hand and the problem should be solved. Be prepared to get your whole arm dirty while performing this task.

Wood Stove Safety

To avoid a fire outside of the stove, be careful of sparks flying from the firebox and avoid keeping dry wood near the stove. Keep curtains and other flammable materials away from the stove and the stove pipe, which can become very hot when venting smoke outside the house.

Air Conditioner Maintenance

Central air conditioners are complex machines, which makes it best to leave repairs to licensed service contractors. However, there are some things you can do to keep your central air conditioning system running well.

- Keep the outdoor condensing unit clear of leaves and other types of yard debris.
- Keep shrubbery away from the condenser.
- Clean the filter two or three times a cooling season. A clogged filter can cause your unit to overheat, which shuts down the system.
- Invite the service contractor to your house at the beginning of each cooling season to tune your system. One important item for the contractor to check is the level of refrigerant. Occasionally it leaks out, which hurts your machine's efficiency.
- If the system won't run, before calling the service contractor make sure to check the temperature setting and the circuit breaker box to see if a circuit has become overloaded.

ENERGY SAVER

Summer Cooling Tips

- Use fans and open windows if the temperature outside is below 82°F (28°C).
- Install an attic fan to blow hot air that collects in the attic outside.
- If you don't need central air conditioning, use individual units for rooms that need cooling. Make sure to check the unit's efficiency rating before making your purchase, and turn off individual units if you plan to be away from the room for long periods of time.
- Clean or replace air conditioning filters once a month.
- Close shades and curtains to keep out daytime sun.
- Never set your thermostat below the desired level in order to cool a hot house more rapidly.
- When you are in the market to purchase air conditioners, heat pumps, or any other appliance, read the energy labels carefully and purchase the most efficient appliance.

Heat Loss

Cause	Remedy	Page
Air Infiltration	Caulk joints	99–100
	Weatherstrip windows and doors	101
	Install storm doors and windows	101
Uninsulated attic	Insulate attic	103

Heating and cooling your home makes up for about 70% of your total energy consumption. With this in mind, let's begin by looking at ways to reduce energy loss.

The first problem to solve is air infiltration. You can test for this problem by moving a lighted candle around doors and window frames. Just be careful not to set your curtains on fire. If the candle dances at a particular spot, that area needs to be caulked or weatherstripped. You can accomplish both jobs easily and inexpensively. By fixing these little problems, it is possible to reduce heat loss by as much as 30%.

Caulking

Caulk is a putty-like substance for filling cracks. Some important areas in your house to caulk include the joints between door frames and siding, the joints between window frames and siding, outside water faucets, other breaks in the outside house surface, and the place where chimney and masonry meet with siding.

<u>Tools to Have on Hand:</u> caulking gun, utility knife

Selecting the right caulk is a daunting task because there are so many different products to choose from. The caulk will need to be waterproof and flexible because the joint will probably expand and contract with changing weather conditions. You will also need to take into account whether the caulk will adhere to aluminum or wood.

Caulks vary greatly in terms of their expense. Ask an experienced salesperson at a hardware or paint supply store to help you choose the right product. Be wary of inexpensive caulks because they do not last

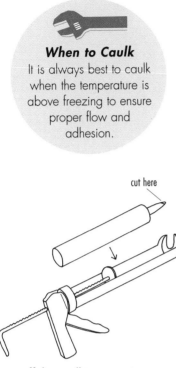

cut here

Cut off the caulking gun tip at a 45-degree angle.

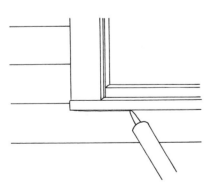

Apply a bead of caulking along all joints around windows and doors.

very long. They also lack flexibility and therefore should not be used in joints that expand and contract.

Once you select your caulk, it is extremely important that you prepare the surface properly.

1. Read the directions on the tube before beginning work because some caulks require that the surface be primed first. In addition, these directions will tell you if you are dealing with toxic substances and should take safety precautions. Clean out dirt, debris, old paint chippings, and loose caulk. If the crack or opening is a large one, use filler material (caulking cotton, sponge rubber, rope, plastic) before completing the job with caulk. Make sure the surface is dry before applying the new caulk.

2. Caulk comes in a tube and is applied with a caulking gun. Use a utility knife to cut the tip of the nozzle at a 45-degree angle. Cutting toward the tip of the nozzle provides for a slower flow or bead of material than cutting further down. It is a good idea to start with a smaller hole than a larger one that will produce too much flow.

3. If you need to keep the caulk off an adjoining surface, stick masking tape to that surface.

4. Next, place the cartridge into the gun, making sure to squeeze the trigger several times to bring the plunger snug up to the cartridge tube. Take a nail or another sharp object to puncture a hole through the open nozzle into the cartridge.

5. You can now gently squeeze the trigger and caulk will begin to ooze out. Move along at a steady pace to maintain a consistent bead.

6. When you are finished, plug the hole in the caulking tube with a large nail.

Weatherstripping

To prevent loss of heat in the winter, windows and doors need to be weatherstripped.

<u>Tools to Have on Hand:</u> straight-slot or Phillips screwdriver (as needed), electric drill (optional)

Windows. The simplest approach is to purchase an adhesive-backed foam at the hardware store. Remove the protective strip of paper from the foam and place the foam along the outside of the bottom sections of the upper and lower window sashes (see drawing at right).

Doors. The same approach is used for sealing doors. Press the tape in place along the inside of the door stop (see drawing at right).

The bottom edge of the door poses a more difficult challenge. The problem is that the door must be able to open and close easily without additional resistance from the seal. If your floor is wood or vinyl, a door sweep can be quite easily installed. A door sweep is a metal or vinyl strip that is attached to the inside of the door with the sweep resting flush against the floor (see drawing, bottom right). If you have thick carpeting or an uneven floor, try installing a special sweep that rises when the door opens and drops when the door is closed. You can purchase such a sweep at a hardware store. If that doesn't solve the problem, you will need to consult with a carpenter.

Storm Windows and Doors

The last defense against air infiltration is adding storm windows and storm doors. If you don't already have storm doors, installing them is a difficult job if you are not a skilled carpenter. Storm windows are easier to install; however, an effective and relatively easy solution is to tape plastic on the inside or outside of your windows. You can purchase special plastic kits for this task at your local hardware store. Follow the directions on the kit and your windows will be airtight.

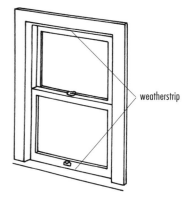

weatherstrip

Apply adhesive-backed foam weatherstrips to top and bottom of window.

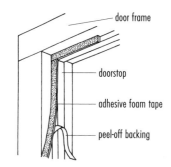

door frame

doorstop

adhesive foam tape

peel-off backing

Secure adhesive-backed foam weatherstrips along top and sides of door frames.

inside of door

Install a door sweep along the bottom edge of the door.

Insulating

Once you are satisfied that your house is protected from air infiltration, it is time to check the insulation. Insulating materials contain millions of tiny air pockets that trap heat trying to pass through. The more air pockets per square inch, the more the material is resistant to heat transfer. This resistance is measured in terms of R-values. The R stands for resistance, and the number indicates the effectiveness of the material in providing resistance. The higher the number, the more effective the material is for resisting heat transfer. (See pages 186–188 for more specifics.)

Fiberglass Insulation. Fiberglass is the most common insulation and it comes in two forms. The first type, batt, consists of rock wool or fluffy fiberglass. It comes in 4- to 8-foot lengths with a width of 15 to 23 inches. It is commonly used to insulate rafters, crawl spaces, walls, ceilings, and unfinished attic floors, and is both moisture- and fire-resistant. The second type, called blanket, is very similar to batt. The only difference between them is that blanket insulation comes in continuous rolls, which makes for less waste but more difficult handling.

Loose-Fill Insulation. Loose-fill insulation is either blown or poured. Poured insulation is especially good for attics with irregular spacing between the joists or when there are many obstructions to work around. Blown insulation is used for closed spaces such as ceilings, walls, and floors. These insulations come in a variety of materials, including fiberglass, rock wool, and cellulose.

Foam Insulation. Foam insulation is also used to insulate finished ceilings, walls, and floors (closed spaces). Once the foam is injected into an empty space it hardens, providing an excellent R-value. The problem is that it is the most expensive type and you will need to hire a professional to do the job.

Rigid Insulation. Rigid insulation consists of boards made of polystyrene. It is excellent for insulating roofs, ceilings, foundation basement walls — wherever you need a thin, high R-value material. The only problem with this type of insulation is that it is highly flammable. Thus, it is important to face the material with drywall for fire protection.

Insulating the Attic

Because heat rises, a poorly insulated attic is a major cause of heat loss. You can save 25% of your heating costs by completely insulating your attic.

<u>Tools to Have on Hand:</u> hammer, sheet of plywood, utility knife

If your attic is to remain unfinished, insulate the floor in order to keep heat in the house below. If you plan to turn it into a room, insulate the walls and ceiling but not the floor, so heat can rise up from the house. Be sure not to insulate the attic vents. They let hot air out in the summer and keep air circulating in the winter to prevent vapor build-up.

For this job, use either blanket or batt fiberglass insulation. You can determine the amount you will need by multiplying the length of the area by its width. Multiply it again by .90 to take into account space taken up by joists and rafters. If the joists come at intervals of 24 inches on center, multiply the square footage by .94.

Preventing Water Condensation

Water condensation happens when warm, moist air comes in contact with the cold air in the attic. To avoid this problem, blanket and batt insulation come with a vapor barrier. This is the plastic or paper sheet to which the fiberglass is attached. If you are laying loose insulation, you will need a sheet of plastic to serve as a vapor barrier.

The vapor barrier is always placed so that it faces the warm air. When laying insulation on an attic floor with open joists, place the vapor barrier directly onto the floor. Start at one end and insert the insulation between the joists on top of the vapor barrier. It may help to use a sheet of plywood to kneel on if the attic is without a floor.

If you are adding to insulation with a vapor barrier, purchase new insulation that is "unfaced," or without a barrier. You do not want moisture to build up between the two layers of insulation.

To lay insulation on unfinished walls or the ceiling, place it between the joists or rafters with the vapor barrier facing the attic floor. Secure the insulation in place with wire fasteners slightly bigger than the joists. Insert these wires between the joists about every three feet (see drawing at right). Remember not to cover the attic vents.

SAFETY TIP

Asbestos Alert

Always wear a mask in addition to protective clothing. If old insulation is in place, it may contain asbestos. There is no need to remove it if the old insulation is in good shape, but the fact that asbestos dust is a prime cause of lung cancer is a very good reason to wear that mask.

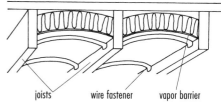

joists   wire fastener   vapor barrier

Lay insulation between joists with the vapor barrier facing the attic floor.

Chapter Five

Windows and Doors

Windows and Doors

AT A GLANCE

- broken windowpanes
- jammed windows
- swollen doors
- dead bolt locks

and more

Windows

PROBLEM	CAUSE	REMEDY	PAGE
Broken windowpane		Replace pane in wooden window	107–108
		Replace pane in aluminum window	110
		Replace pane in horizontal sliding window	110
Sliding window not sliding properly	Dent in track	Repair track	110
Stuck double-hung windows	Sealed with paint	Cut dried paint with knife	111
		Push up window frame	111
		Hammer latch	111
	Expanded wood	Lubricate window	112
		Enlarge sash groove, plane sashes	112
Broken double-hung window cord or chain		Replace cord or chain	112
Stuck casement windows	Dirt obstructing window movement	Clean metal arm	113
Crank handle stuck		Oil crank handle	113
Handle gears obstructed		Clean and lubricate handle gears	113

Fixing Broken Windowpanes

There are many different types of windows. Some are wood and some are aluminum. There are double-hung windows, casement windows, horizontal sliding windows, awning and jalousie windows. No matter what kind of window you have, one of the most common problems is a broken pane.
<u>Tool to Have on Hand:</u> duct tape

   Temporary Fix. If you don't want to fix a broken windowpane yourself and the repairperson can't promise you when he or she will get around to it, the best solution is a temporary repair.

   1. While wearing protective gloves, pull out the glass that is easily removed from the window frame.

2. Using heavy-gauge plastic, cover the window from the outside and attach the plastic to the frame with duct tape.

3. To provide extra protection from the cold, cut a piece of cardboard and place it inside the window frame from the inside. Then cover the inside frame with plastic and secure it to the frame with duct tape. That should do it until the repairperson comes around.

Replacing Broken Panes. If you want to avoid the repairperson, replacing a broken pane of glass is not a difficult task and it can save you lots of money. The project varies slightly with each type of window. First, the broken glass must be removed — carefully. In a wooden window it is often held in place by a layer of putty (a clay-like substance) and glazier's points (small metal triangles with sharp points).

<u>Tools to Have on Hand:</u> putty knife, pliers, straight-slot screwdriver

1. Scrape away the old putty with a kitchen knife or putty knife (see drawing at right).

2. Next, pull away the broken pieces of glass. Make sure to wear protective gloves so you don't cut yourself.

3. You will probably see three or four glazier's points inserted into the wood, which can be pulled out with pliers. Some window panes are held in place by small wooden slats which are nailed into place. These slats need to be pried out.

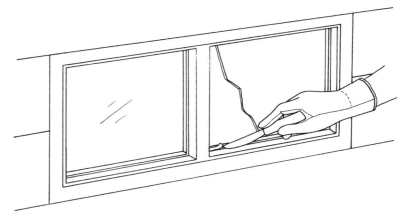

Steps 1–2: Scrape away the old putty and carefully remove the broken glass.

4. Once you have cleaned around the lip of the wooden frame, take an exact measurement of the frame. Write down the length and width so you don't forget the dimensions. At a hardware store or glass company, purchase a new glass pane. Have it cut to fit ⅛ inch smaller than each dimension of your frame. You will also need to buy a small can of putty and some glazier's points.

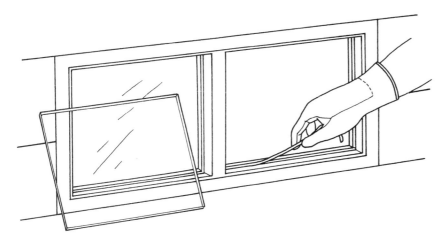

Step 5: Run a bead of putty all the way around the frame.

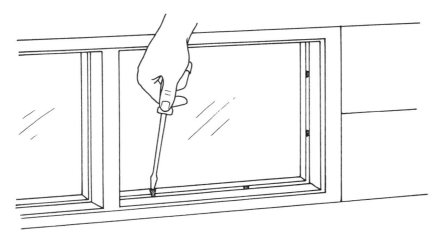

Step 7: Push glazier point in with a screwdriver.

5. Thinly layer the window frame with putty.

6. Gently push the new glass into place. It should fit snugly up against the lip of the frame.

7. To hold the glass in place, insert a glazier's point along each side of the window frame. Hold the glazier's point right next to the glass and push it into the frame with a straight-slot screwdriver or a putty knife. The point is sharp and should go in easily.

8. Now you need to seal the window tight with an additional layer of putty. The best way to do this is to take a handful of putty and shape it into a ball. Rub the putty ball between your hands until the putty takes the shape of a snake. Press the snake along the edges of the glass, which forms the seal. Finally, smooth over the putty with your putty knife, removing any excess putty from the glass.

Replacing Glazing Compound

The glazing compound that holds your windowpanes in place and seals out moisture becomes brittle and cracks with age. This leads to air drafts entering the house and moisture, which can damage the window sash.

<u>Tools to Have on Hand:</u> putty knife, paint brush

1. To solve the problem, remove all the old, loose compound with a putty knife. Be careful not to disturb the triangular glazier's points that hold the pane in place.

2. Roll new glazing compound or putty in your hands to form a long snake and press it against the windowpane.

3. Take a putty knife and run it along the snake at a 45-degree angle, pressing it against the pane as you proceed.

4. Paint over the glazing compound to complete your seal.

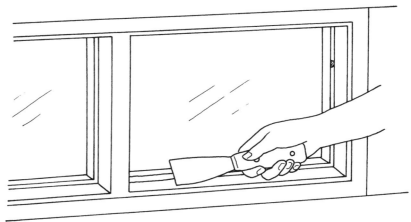

Step 3: Press glazing compound against pane with putty knife.

Step 3: Replace the gasket by pushing it in place with your thumb.

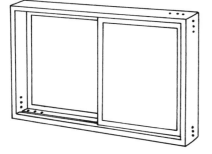

To repair aluminum sliding windows, you may have to remove the entire pane by unfastening the screws at the top, bottom, and sides.

Repairing Aluminum Windows

If you are repairing aluminum windows, the panes are usually held in place by a rubber gasket.

1. Pull the gasket out and remove the pieces of glass.
2. Have a piece of glass cut $\frac{1}{32}$ of an inch smaller than the frame.
3. Lay the new pane in the frame and replace the gasket with your thumb.

Replacing Horizontal Sliding Windows

Horizontal sliding windows move from side to side rather than up and down. The window sash slides along a metal track. You can replace the broken glass by taking apart the aluminum frame.

<u>Tools to Have on Hand:</u> straight-slot or Phillips screwdriver

1. Take out the screws or pins that hold the upper and bottom rails to the sides. This will disassemble the window.
2. Remove the pieces of glass and lay the new pane in the frame. Assemble one side at a time and secure the entire frame with the screws or pins.

Unfortunately, the instructions above apply mainly to older windows. Newer models, especially aluminum ones, are manufactured in such a way that it is impossible for you to disassemble the window frame. If this is the case, you will need to remove the entire sash and bring it to a glass company for replacement. The only consolation is that your newer window is probably far more energy efficient than the older models.

Repairing Sliding Glass Windows

Problems with sliding glass windows are usually found in the lower track.

<u>Tool to Have on Hand:</u> hammer (as needed)

If your window does not slide smoothly, clean out the debris in the track and lubricate it with paraffin or silicone lube. In your examination of the track, you may find that it is bent. To solve this problem, cut a wooden block that fits snugly into the track. Insert the block into the bent area and gently tap the bent area with a hammer. That should solve it.

Unsticking Double-Hung Windows

If you have double-hung windows that will not open or close easily, it is helpful to understand how this type of window is constructed. There is an upper and lower sash. The upper sash lies outside the lower one, and both move up and down. This movement is regulated by pulleys and cords within the sides of the window (see drawing at right).

There are several reasons why these windows stick. Windows that are painted often become stuck and refuse to open. The trick is to move the window up and down before the paint is completely dry. If you forget to do this and end up with a window that won't move, it is not too difficult to remedy.

Tools to Have on Hand: sharp kitchen knife, hammer (as needed)

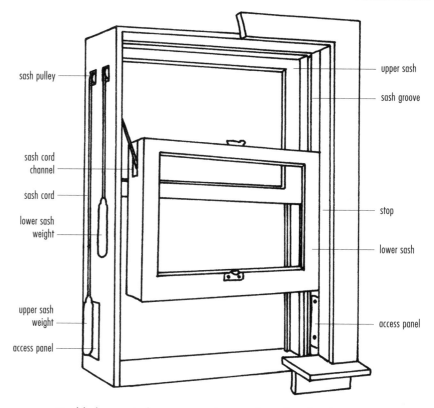

upper sash

sash groove

sash pulley

sash cord channel

sash cord

lower sash weight

stop

lower sash

upper sash weight

access panel

access panel

Double-hung windows operate by a sash cord and pulley system.

Unsticking Painted Windows.

1. Try taking a sharp kitchen knife and running it along the edges of the window. Your goal is to cut through the dried paint. Try to open the window again.

2. You may be lucky, but if it still won't budge, place your palms on the window frame and push up hard. Be careful that your hands don't slip and go through the glass.

3. As a last resort, take a block of wood and place it directly under the metal locking latch. Then take a hammer and gently tap up. That should do it.

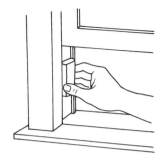

Rub paraffin or soap along the
inside of the sash groove.

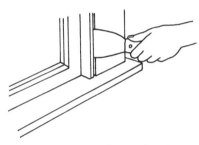

Step 1: Remove the inside strip on
the side of the sash groove.

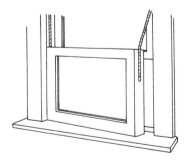

Step 3: Lift out the sash.

Unsticking Expanded Windows. Another cause of windows sticking is when humidity and moisture expand the wood in the window. In this case you need to either lubricate the window or enlarge the sash groove.

<u>Tool to Have on Hand:</u> hammer (as needed)

• To lubricate the window, rub paraffin or hard soap along the inside of the sash groove (see drawing at left).

• To enlarge the sash groove, take a block of wood the width of the sash and put it into the sash groove. Tap the block of wood along the length of the groove to expand the frame.

Planing Window Sashes. The most drastic approach, and a last resort, is to dismantle the window and plane the sides to fit the groove.

<u>Tools to Have on Hand:</u> straight-slot or Phillips screwdriver, plane

1. To take the sashes out of the frame, first remove the inside strip on the side of the sash groove. This will allow you to move the lower sash sideways and raise it above the window sill enough to clear the frame. The sash will be attached to a cord or a chain.

2. Remove the cord or chain and ease the cord up to the pulley.

3. Lift out the sash.

4. You can now remove the upper sash in the same manner.

5. Plane the sides of the sash so that they will have enough clearance in the groove to slide easily.

6. When you have finished planing, replace the window by reversing these instructions.

Replacing the Window Cord or Chain

If you have a broken cord or chain in your window, you must remove the sash as described above. In some windows, it is necessary to remove the frame to expose the weight attached to the cord or chain. In other windows, there is a place for the weight inside the frame. The weight can be exposed by removing the screws holding the cover in place (see drawing at right).

<u>Tools to Have on Hand:</u> straight-slot or Phillips screwdriver

1. Remove the weight and the cord or chain from the sash.
2. Cut a piece of replacement cord or chain and reattach the weight.
3. Reassemble the cord or chain through the pulley and fasten it to the sash in the same way as you removed it.
4. Reassemble the window and frame.

Opening Stuck Casement Windows

<u>Tools to Have on Hand:</u> straight-slot or Phillips screwdriver

1. If you are having problems opening and closing a casement window, first check the arm, the thin metal piece that enables the window to slide in and out.
2. Remove any grease, paint, or object that is interfering with the window's ability to move freely along the arm's surface.
3. If the arm is in good shape, the problem is probably with the crank. Apply a few drops of oil to the crank handle and see if that helps.
4. If not, you will need to dismantle the crank and check its internal parts. This is easily done by taking out the screws that hold it to the window frame.
5. Once you have removed the crank, examine the gears to see if anything is obstructing them.
6. Clean the gears, remove any obstructions, and oil them with a multipurpose lubricant. If you find that the gears are stripped or badly worn, you will need to replace the entire crank mechanism.

Opening Stuck Awning Windows

An awning window is a casement window that opens from the top out. When such a window becomes stuck, it is fixed the same way as a casement window is, as described above.

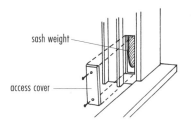

Step 1: Access the weight by removing the cover under the strip.

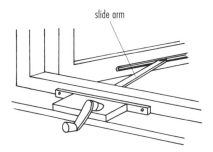

Step 1: Check to see that the slide arm is free of dirt and grease.

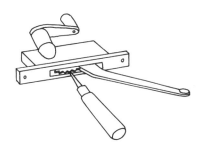

Step 6: Clean the gears.

Screen Windows and Doors

PROBLEM	REMEDY	PAGE
Torn screen	Replace screen	114–115
Hole in screen	Patch screen	115

Replacing Screens

<u>Tools to Have on Hand</u>: straight-slot screwdriver, scissors, staple gun (optional), small hammer (as needed)

Screens are attached to window and door frames in many different ways. Some are hooked onto the sill, some have spring-loaded plugs, and others slide in and out.

1. To repair a torn screen, figure out which type you have and remove it accordingly.

2. Once this task is accomplished, take the screen away from the window or door and lay it on a table.

If the window frame or door is wooden, you will notice that the screen is held in place by a narrow molding. This molding must be pried off so that the screen can be taken out. Take a straight-slot screwdriver and pry up gently. You want to avoid splitting or breaking the molding. The small nails or staples holding the molding in place should yield to your gentle prying. If the molding breaks, it is not a major disaster because it can be inexpensively replaced. Take out the screen and remove as many tacks or staples from the molding as you can.

If you have a metal window or door frame, your task is somewhat simpler. The molding that fastens the screen to the frame is actually a thin rubber hose or gasket. To remove the damaged screen, take your screwdriver, pry up the gasket and pull it out.

3. Take the screen out and measure the frame.

4. Take the dimensions of the frame to the hardware store and ask that they cut you a section of screen to fit your frame. There are different types of screens to choose from, so you will need to ask a knowledgeable

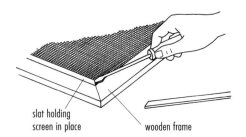

slat holding
screen in place

wooden frame

Wooden frame: Pry off the molding strip to expose the screen edge.

salesperson about the best type to suit your needs. You may have to buy a roll of screen and cut the piece yourself. Scissors will cut the screen easily. It is best to leave 1½ to 2 inches extra on each side.

5. Fold this excess screen over to form a reinforced edge on each side.

6. ***With a wooden window or door frame,*** place the new screen into the frame and attach it with carpet tacks or by using a staple gun. Make sure you stretch the screen tightly so that it does not sag. Now replace the old molding and the job is finished.

With a metal window or door frame, install the new screen by placing it on the frame. Next, take the gasket and put it back into place while pushing the screen into the indented track. Be careful not to tear the screen. An inexpensive tool is available for pushing the gasket back into the track. It can be purchased at your local hardware store.

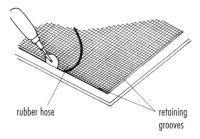

rubber hose | retaining grooves

Metal frame: The gasket is pushed back into place with a special tool.

Patching Screens

A small hole in a screen can be easily patched. This is a cheap and easy solution, but it is not always aesthetically pleasing.

Tool to Have on Hand: scissors

1. Go to the hardware store and purchase the smallest section of screen that you can.

2. Using a pair of scissors, cut a patch from this screen about an inch or two larger than the hole.

3. Unravel the edges of the screen patch by pulling out a few wires. Bend the ends of the remaining wires along the edges of the patch area so that they are at a 90-degree angle to the patch.

4. Place the patch over the hole with the wire ends sticking through the regular screen holes.

5. Bend the wire ends back into the screen so that they hold the patch firmly in place.

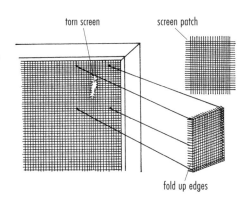

torn screen | screen patch | fold up edges

Cut a small patch, fold up the edges, place patch over hole, and bend wire ends into the back of the screen.

Doors

PROBLEM	CAUSE	REMEDY	PAGE
Bi-fold doors do not fit together	Improperly installed, wood expanded or contracted	Adjust doors	116–117
Door doesn't lock or stay closed	Faulty doorknob	Replace doorknob	117
	Door hinges loose or bent	Tighten or replace hinges	118
	Hinges pulled away from wall	Reinsert screws with wooden matches or use larger screws	118
		Move strike plate	118
Door lock sticks		Lubricate lock with WD-40	118
Door squeaks		Lubricate hinges with WD-40	118
Stuck wooden doors	Loose hinges	Tighten hinges	119
		Adjust screw holes	119
		Insert shim	119
	Moisture	Wait for weather change	118
		Sand or plane doors	119

Fixing Bi-Fold Doors

If you have bi-fold doors in a closet that do not fit together properly because they were improperly installed or have expanded or contracted, you can easily fix the problem by adjusting the doors.

1. The first step is to remove the doors. Simply lift up gently and pull the bottom of the door. This will enable the plastic pins that move along the track-like door frame to come out, which frees the door.

2. A pin on the bottom corner of the door nearest to the wall sits on a small metal track on the floor and is adjustable. It screws in and out to adjust the height of the door. Set the pin at the desired height and then put the door back on its track. This is done by first inserting the top plastic pins in the upper metal track. You will note that there is a holding device inserted into the metal track nearest the wall. This device has a hole in it to hold the inside plastic pin. The other plastic pin fits in the

track. Insert the two pins by pushing the door up while making sure that the pin nearest the wall goes into the little hole. While the door is held up, direct it to its proper alignment along the wall and insert the metal pin on the bottom of the door into its track on the floor (see drawing at right).

3. The width of the door is adjusted by moving the holding device. This device is held in place by a screw. Loosen the screw by turning it counterclockwise and slide the holding device to the desired position. Note that you cannot move it farther from the wall than the corresponding metal track on the floor. Replace the door as described above.

Replacing a Doorknob

A door that is difficult to lock or refuses to stay shut may have a faulty doorknob. You may have either of the following kinds of doorknobs:

Type 1 — two screws on the inside knob hold the entire mechanism in place. Unfasten these screws and slip off the knob that is not fastened to the mechanism. You will see the doorknob mechanism on the inside. After unscrewing the two screws, slip the entire mechanism out.

Type 2 — a stem with a latch within the knob holds the doorknob in place. You will notice a small hole in the stem. Push a sharp tool into the hole while pulling the doorknob off. The rest of the mechanism will slide out from the other side. Unscrew the latch mechanism and slide it out (see drawing at right).

<u>Tools to Have on Hand:</u> straight-slot or Phillips screwdriver, compass or ice pick (as needed)

1. Take the old doorknob to the hardware store and purchase the type of doorknob that you want.

2. Read the directions for the new doorknob before installing it.

3. The first thing to install is the latch mechanism — the last thing you took off when removing the broken doorknob. This part will screw into the end of the door. Make sure the rounded part is toward the door opening. If you install it the other way, the door will not stay shut.

4. Once the latch mechanism is in place, take both sides of the doorknob and insert them into the latch mechanism. You will have to depress the latch for the doorknob to fit into the slot in the middle. Screw in the two screws that fasten the doorknob to the door.

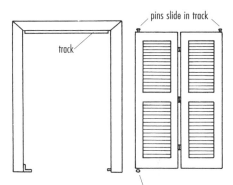

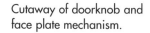

Lift doors up to release pins from track at top of door.

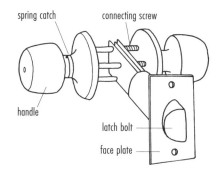

Cutaway of doorknob and face plate mechanism.

Fixing a Door Latch/Strike Plate

A misaligned door latch and strike plate may also cause a door not to shut or remain closed.

<u>Tools to Have on Hand:</u> straight-slot or Phillips screwdriver, chisel (as needed), hammer (as needed)

1. Check to see whether the hinges have loosened or become bent.
2. If they have, tighten them or replace them if necessary.
3. If they have pulled away from the wall, try sticking wooden matchsticks into the holes and then reinserting the screws. If this does not work, you will have to find a new place for the hinges, or try larger screws.

Another solution to this problem is to move the strike plate.

1. Unscrew the strike plate from the door jamb, take a chisel, and cut away a small section in the direction you need to move the strike plate.
2. Screw the strike plate into its new position. You may also need to enlarge the hole into which the latch mechanism is inserted.

Sticky Locks

Does the lock on your door stick, making it difficult to unlock? Don't try to solve the problem by using excessive force with your key. This will only break the key, which will require installing a new lock. Instead spray WD-40 around the latch and turn the doorknob several times to work the lubricant into the lock mechanism.

Squeaky Doors

Doors that squeak are annoying but easily fixed. Take a can of WD-40 and squirt the hinges. This should stop the squeak.

Hard-to-Open Wooden Doors

Doors may become difficult to open and close when the hinges are out of alignment. A sagging hinge or one in which the leaves are not recessed flush with the door jamb will throw the door out of alignment.

Wooden doors are also sensitive to the amount of moisture in the air. Too much moisture tends to make them swell, while too little causes them to shrink. When it rains a lot, wooden doors may become difficult to open

Planing Tips
Plane slowly from door edge toward center so as not to split or chip the corner of the door. Remove wood in thin shavings.

and close. When the rain subsides, they may or may not return to their actual size, and may have to be sanded or planed.

Adjusting the Hinges. If your door is sticking, the first place to look is the hinges.

<u>Tools to Have on Hand:</u> straight-slot or Phillips screwdriver, electric drill (as needed), sandpaper (as needed), plane (as needed), chisel (as needed), hammer (as needed)

Tighten any loose screws, which will prevent the door from sagging. If you cannot tighten the screws because the holes have enlarged, drive a wedge under the outside edge of the door to support it. Take out the hinge screws, fill the holes with glue, and then insert scrap wood or wooden matchsticks into the holes. After the glue has dried, drive the screws into the old holes. You may need to drill a small hole to accomplish this task.

If the door sticks at the top or bottom, you may be able to fix the problem by placing a cardboard shim (a thin piece of cardboard about the size of a credit card) behind the hinge leaf in the door jamb. Shim the top hinge for a door that sticks at the top and the bottom hinge for one that sticks at the bottom. With the weight of the door supported by a wedge inserted under the outside edge, unscrew the hinge leaf in the door jamb, place the shim in the recessed space of the door jamb, replace the hinge leaf, and screw it back into the door jamb with the screws going through the shim and then into the holes in the door jamb.

Sanding or Planing the Door. The other way to solve the problem of a hard-to-open wooden door is by sanding or planing the door.

1. Close the door and see how it fits by sliding a business card between the door and the jamb. Wherever the card sticks, mark the door with a pencil.

2. Sand or plane the door in the places marked by the pencil. Use sandpaper if the problem area is a small one. It saves a great deal of time to keep the door in place while planing or sanding. You need only remove the door to work on the side where the hinges are located or to work on the bottom of the door.

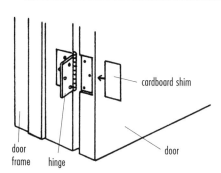

Place a cardboard shim in the recessed space of the door jamb.

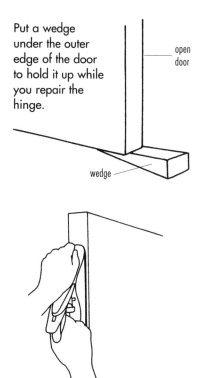

Put a wedge under the outer edge of the door to hold it up while you repair the hinge.

Step 2: Plane from the edge of the door toward the center.

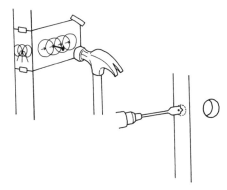

Use a template to determine where to drill for a new dead-bolt.

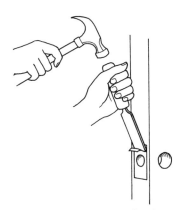

Chisel out the mortise cut for the latch plate.

Installing Dead-Bolt Locks

<u>Tools to Have on Hand:</u> electric drill, specialty drill bits, hammer, chisel, straight-slot or Phillips screwdriver

Dead-bolt locks provide an inexpensive way to add security to your home. They are not difficult to install if you have the necessary equipment. The most important item is a set of specialty drill bits for drilling large holes. Before purchasing the lock, measure the thickness of the door so that you buy the right size lock.

1. Drill two large holes in the door where the lock is to be placed.

2. A template comes with the lock, which indicates where to drill the two holes. Tape the template onto the door in the place where you want to position the lock (see drawing at left).

3. Using a specialty drill bit for drilling large holes (the directions that come with the lock will specify the correct drill bit size), drill a hole through your door as indicated on the template. To avoid splintering the door frame, stop drilling as soon as the bit breaks through to the other side. Finish the job from the other side.

4. Drill a smaller hole starting from the door's edge into the larger hole. Again, the exact location of the hole will be marked on the template. This smaller hole is the one that the bolt will travel through.

5. You are now ready to insert the dead bolt and its latch plate. The latch plate must be recessed into the edge of the door frame with a mortise cut. With the lock in place, draw an outline of the latch plate with a pencil on the door's edge. You now need to chisel out the mortise cut.

6. Take a hammer and tap the chisel along your outline. Be careful not to cut deeper into the wood than the thickness of your strike plate.

7. While holding the chisel at a 45-degree angle, make a series of cuts that run from the top of the plate to the bottom (see drawing at left).

8. Work out the chips by tapping your chisel from the side of the door frame. Lay the latch plate into the mortise cut to see if it fits. You may need to fine-tune your cut to ensure that it lies flush.

9. Once you are satisfied with the position of the plate, screw it in.

10. You can now finish assembling the lock. Follow the directions that come with the lock.

11. Install the strike plate on the door jamb. This will involve making another mortise cut into which the strike plate fits as well as drilling a hole for the dead bolt. In some cases, the drilling of this last hole is all that is required. To ensure that this last hole is correctly positioned, apply lipstick or wet paint to the end of the bolt. Now close the door and move the bolt snugly up against the jamb. This will mark where the hole needs to be. You have now successfully installed a dead-bolt lock.

Installing Curtain Rods

There are two basic curtain rods — an adjustable stationary rod and an adjustable traverse rod. If you envision frequent adjustment of the curtains, I strongly recommend the traverse rod. Either rod can be purchased from the hardware store and installation is a simple job.

<u>Tools to Have on Hand:</u> straight-slot or Phillips screwdriver, electric drill, hammer (as needed)

1. Begin by placing the brackets that hold the rod at the upper corners of the window trim. Do not install the brackets in plaster or wallboard because these materials will not support the weight of the curtains. Be careful not to nail or screw the rod holder into the joint of the frame or too close to the corner of the frame.

2. Mark through the holes of the brackets with a pencil, and drill holes that are slightly smaller than the screws that come with the drapery hardware. If you do not have a drill, take a medium-sized nail and drive it part-way into the place where the screw is to go. Pry out the nail, and you have a hole to start the screw.

3. Screw the brackets into the window trim. If the curtain rod is more than 48 inches long, it is a good idea to insert an additional middle bracket equidistant from the two outer brackets.

4. With the brackets in place, adjust the rod to the correct length, and place it in the brackets. You are now ready to hang curtains.

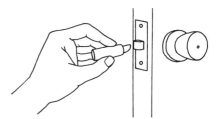

Drilling Help
It often helps when drilling to have a friend hold the door so that it doesn't move while you are working.

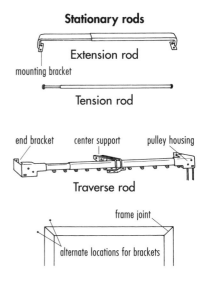

To position the dead bolt properly, apply lipstick or paint to the end of the bolt and move the bolt against the jamb to mark the hole.

Stationary rods

Extension rod

mounting bracket

Tension rod

end bracket   center support   pulley housing

Traverse rod

frame joint

alternate locations for brackets

Chapter Six

Walls

AT A GLANCE

- hanging pictures
- repairing holes
- wallpapering
- painting
and more

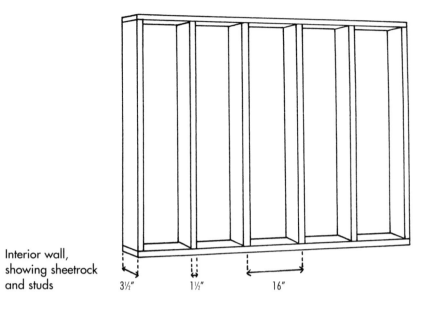

Interior wall, showing sheetrock and studs

3½" 1½" 16"

There is nothing that brightens up a room more than an attractive picture, a fresh coat of paint, or a pretty wallpaper pattern. In order to accomplish projects of this type, it is necessary to understand how walls are constructed.

Most interior walls are constructed with sheetrock and studs. The studs are vertical pieces of wood that provide a framework for the wall. They are usually 1½ inches thick, 3½ inches deep, and spaced every 16 or 24 inches on center along the wall. The term "on center" means that the 16- or 24-inch measurement is taken from the center of one stud to the center of the next one, making the empty space between studs slightly less than the 16 or 24 inches (see drawing above). The sheetrock — a plaster panel with a heavy cardboard backing — is nailed to the studs to form the wall.

It is important to understand wall construction when hanging things. The main principle is that sheetrock, by itself, cannot support the hanging of a heavy item such as a mirror. A heavy mirror must be hung from a nail that has been inserted into a stud.

Hanging Objects on Walls

PROBLEM	REMEDY	PAGE
Lightweight objects	Use picture-hanging hook	125
Medium-weight objects	Use toggle bolt or molly bolt	125
Heavy objects	Insert screw or nail into wall stud	126
Concrete walls	Drill hole and insert anchor	127

Hanging Lightweight Objects

Many items can be hung on the wall without worrying about the studs. For example, a lightweight picture can be placed anywhere.

<u>Tool to Have on Hand:</u> small hammer

Purchase a picture-hanging hook (they come in various sizes depending on the size of the picture) from the hardware store. The hook comes with a small nail, which is inserted through the hook and into the wall at an angle (see drawing at right).

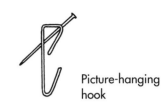

Picture-hanging hook

Hanging Medium-Weight Objects

To hang a small mirror requires more support and a somewhat different approach.

<u>Tools to Have on Hand:</u> electric drill, straight-slot screwdriver

There are many easy-to-use products on the market for attaching items to sheetrock and other types of walls.

Toggle Bolt. A toggle bolt is a bolt with wings on it. These wings, operated by springs, fan out behind the sheetrock to provide additional support (see drawing at right).

1. Begin by drilling a hole into the wall. The size of the hole will be specified on the toggle bolt.

2. Remove the folded wings from the toggle bolt and insert the bolt through the object to be hung. Replace the wings onto the bolt, making sure that they are in a folded position and facing the object to be hung.

3. Push the toggle bolt through the hole.

4. Turn the bolt with a screwdriver to cause the wings to fan out behind the sheetrock and provide your hanger with a secure grip on the wall. You may have to pull on the bolt to snug the wings up to the back of the wall in order to tighten it.

Molly Bolt. Another type of fastener is the molly bolt. Using one also requires a hole to be drilled in the wall. Insert the molly bolt into the hole and turn the screw clockwise to expand the bolt and secure it to the wall (see drawing at right).

Hanging on Hollow Doors

On a hollow door, use a hollow door anchor, which is like a molly bolt but is used for a thinner surface.

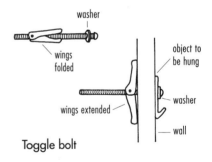

Toggle bolt

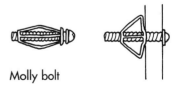

Molly bolt

Hanging Heavy Objects

For a heavy mirror or wall clock, it is best to fasten the hanger into a stud. This presents the interesting problem of finding the stud. Remember that studs are generally 1½ inches wide and are located every 16 inches on center across your wall.

<u>Tools to Have on Hand:</u> stud finder (optional), hammer, straight-slot screwdriver, electric drill (optional), tape measure (as needed)

There are four ways to locate studs:

• Purchase a stud finder from the hardware store. This finder locates the nail connecting the sheetrock to the stud through magnetism. It should be noted, however, that this method is neither foolproof nor cheap.

• Locate the nail holes in the molding where the floor and wall meet. These are often located at the stud.

• Gently tap your knuckles against the sheetrock. Here's how to do it: Go to the corner of the wall where you can be assured of finding a stud and gently tap. Move six inches along the wall and tap again. Here, the sheetrock unsupported by a stud should have a slightly different sound and a more hollow feel. Move along the wall to the approximate place you want to hang the heavy object and tap gently, listening for the sound and feel of the stud.

When you think you have located it, drive a very thin nail into the wall to see if it strikes the stud. If it doesn't, try inserting the nail one inch to either side of where you first inserted the nail. If you miss the stud, start tapping again.

• Find an outlet or a switch. There will be a stud on one side of these boxes. Drive a thin nail into the sheetrock on either side of the outlet or switch to locate the stud. Once you've found it, measure 16-inch increments to the stud where you want to hang your object.

Once the stud is located, drive a nail or screw into the stud. Make sure that the nail or screw is large enough to support the object. If you decide to use a screw, begin by drilling a hole into the sheetrock and stud. It is a good idea to make the hole slightly narrower than the width of the screw so that the screw threads grip into the wood.

Hanging Objects on Concrete Walls

If you plan to renovate an unfinished basement into a workshop or family room, you will probably have to fasten objects like shelves or clocks to a concrete or cement block wall. In order to accomplish this task, you will have to drill a hole in the wall and insert an anchor.

<u>Tools to Have on Hand:</u> electric drill, carbide-tipped masonry bit, safety goggles and mask, awl, straight-slot screwdriver (as needed), hammer (as needed)

The first decision to make is whether to use your own ⅜-inch portable electric drill. It will be fine if you only have a few small holes to drill. Attach a carbide-tipped masonry bit to the drill.

If your project requires that you drill several holes or holes larger than ⅜ inch in diameter, rent a heavy duty, ½-inch drill from a tool rental store. This will keep your smaller drill from overheating. You should also pause briefly after drilling each hole to allow the drill bit to cool. This protects the bit tip.

The package containing the anchors will tell you the diameter of the hole to drill. Drill the hole the same depth as the anchor is long. To ensure that you drill the hole the proper depth, measure the depth of the hole on the drill bit and place a piece of tape on the bit to indicate the stopping point. Use an awl to start the hole, which prevents the bit from wandering, and drill slowly. Be patient. Drilling in concrete is slow work. As the hole enlarges, you can increase the speed of the drill.

Anchors come in two types. For an **expansion anchor**, your screw goes into the anchor, which forces the hinges to expand and hold the anchor tightly against the concrete. For a **drop-in anchor**, you first push it into the hole. Then you insert a setting tool (a large nail will do) into the anchor and hammer the setting tool until the anchor is flush with the concrete wall.

Remove the setting tool and screw your object into the anchor. If you are hanging your object, leave part of the screw exposed so that you can hang it at this point.

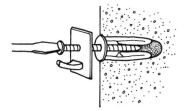

Screw your object into the anchor.

Repairing Holes in Walls

PROBLEM	REMEDY	PAGE
Cracks or small holes	Fill with spackling compound	128
Large holes in plaster walls	Patch with screen and plaster	129
Large holes in sheetrock	Patch with sheetrock; patch with sheetrock and plaster	130–131

Repairing Wall Cracks

<u>Tools to Have on Hand:</u> beer bottle opener (church key), putty knife, fine sandpaper

To repair a crack or small hole in the wall, you will need to purchase a can of spackling compound from a discount, hardware, or paint store and a putty knife about an inch in width.

1. Scrape away any loose plaster along the crack. A good way to handle this problem is to gently run a beer bottle opener along the crack.

2. Scoop the spackling compound onto a putty knife and run the knife over the crack.

3. Allow the compound to harden and then apply another layer of spackling compound to the crack.

4. Continue applying layers until the crack is completely filled.

5. When the final layer is dry, gently sand the repaired surface of the wall using fine sandpaper until it is smooth.

Repairing Large Holes in Plaster Walls

Fixing a large hole in a plaster wall is a little more difficult and time consuming. For plaster walls without lath you will need some plaster, a wire screen, a thin shoelace or wire, and a wooden dowel, thin stick, or pencil that is longer than the width of the hole.

<u>Tools to Have on Hand:</u> scissors, paint brush, putty knife, fine sandpaper

1. Remove all the loose plaster from around the hole.
2. Construct a supporting device within the hole to hold the plaster used for the repair. A good solution is to cut a section of wire screen considerably larger than the hole.
3. Take the shoelace or wire and thread it through the screen. You will use this shoelace to pull the screen tightly against the hole once the screen is inserted.
4. Insert the screen into the hole, pull the shoelace so that the screen fits tightly against the hole, and tie the shoelace to the dowel which you will place across the hole. This will hold the screen in place while you put the first coat of plaster into the hole.
5. To apply the plaster, first moisten the hole and screen with water using a paint brush. Insert enough plaster into the hole so that it oozes into the screen and covers the sides of the hole.
6. When the plaster is thoroughly dry, remove the dowel and the shoelace.
7. Now apply several coats of plaster can be applied to the hole.
8. When the hole is fully covered and dry, sand the area smooth.
9. Apply a priming coat of paint before rolling on the finishing coat.

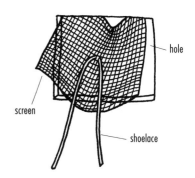

Step 3: Thread shoelace through a wire screen, and push the screen through the hole.

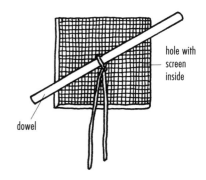

Step 4: Tie a dowel to the screen with the lace.

Repairing Holes in Sheetrock

There are two ways to fix a large hole in sheetrock. One method requires you to enlarge the hole to extend to a stud on each side. The other method involves gluing a sheetrock patch against a plywood backing. In either case, you must first purchase a piece of sheetrock from a building supply store.

<u>Tools to Have on Hand:</u> small saw, large knife (optional), hammer, straight-slot screwdriver (as needed), putty knife, fine sandpaper

Method 1.

1. Take a small saw or large knife and cut a rectangle out around the hole. Make sure that the rectangle extends to a stud on either side.

2. Measure this rectangular hole and cut the new piece of sheetrock with the same dimensions.

3. Nail the patch into the hole by securing it to both studs.

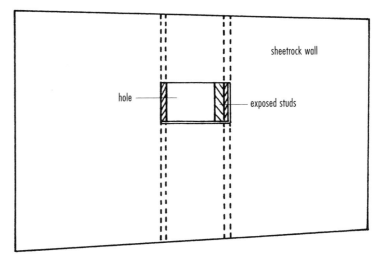

Patch a large hole by screwing a new piece of sheetrock to studs on either side of the hole.

Method 2.

1. Take a new piece of sheetrock and, using a small saw, cut it into a rectangular shape that is larger than the hole in the wall.

2. Place the patch over the hole and outline the patch with a pencil. Take a small saw and cut an opening in the wall along the penciled line.

3. Construct the backing, by first cutting a piece of plywood that is larger than the patch but that can be diagonally inserted into the hole.

4. Insert a small screw into the middle of the plywood, leaving enough space on the screw head to attach a string.

5. Place rubber-based or plastic glue along the border of the plywood and then insert it diagonally into the hole.

6. Attach a string to the small screw so that the plywood can be pulled flush against the wall.

7. While holding the string, drill three or four screws through the sheetrock and into the plywood. The black, all-purpose drywall screws are the best ones for this. Use screws at least 1¼ inches long.

8. Allow the glue about an hour to dry and you are ready to insert the patch. Apply joint compound to the sides and back of the patch and then gently fit it up against the plywood.

9. Use a putty knife to fill the outline cracks with joint compound and then cover the entire surface with it.

10. When the repaired area is dry, lightly sand it.

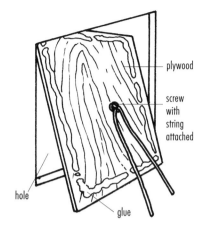

Steps 3–6: Cut a piece of plywood larger than the hole, place a screw at the center, and attach a piece of string to the screw.

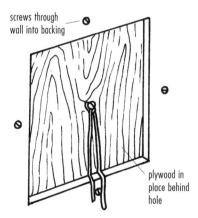

Step 7: Use the string to pull the glued piece of plywood against the hole.

Preparing Walls for Paint

A good paint finish depends on proper wall preparation.

<u>Tools to Have on Hand:</u> putty knife or paint scraper, sandpaper, paint brushes, straight-slot or Phillips screwdriver (as needed)

1. Dust the walls and remove any spots. Paint does not adhere well if there is dust or oil on the walls. Wash each wall with water mixed with a household detergent. Make sure to allow enough time for the walls to dry thoroughly before you start to paint.

2. If there are signs of mildew stains, you will need to do more than merely wash off the stains. Mildew is a live, tiny organism that grows on warm, moist, dark surfaces. If the conditions are right, the mildew you washed off will reappear all too quickly. You need to use an effective cleaning solution to kill those tiny organisms before painting. A good cleaning solution is a mixture of one part bleach to four parts water. For heavy stains, use one part bleach and three parts water. Wear gloves to protect your hands while washing the mildew stains. Allow the wall to dry for thirty-two hours before applying paint. Once the area is properly cleaned, apply a paint with mildewcide.

3. Chipped paint must be scraped and the wall surface sanded smooth. You should also sand any splinters on a wood wall. Painting over knotholes with shellac will help prevent the sap from seeping out and ruining your new paint.

4. Finally, remove all switch and outlet plates.

Painting over Wallpaper

Painting over a wallpapered wall can be done, but it is important to know that the wallpaper will be difficult to remove later. If you decide to paint anyway, the finished job will look better if you first take these steps.

<u>Tools to Have on Hand:</u> scissors, razor or utility knife

1. Wash the paper with warm water and a household detergent to get rid of grease and wall markings.

2. Cut off any loose pieces of paper and sand the edges smooth.

3. Cut open any blisters, glue the edges back to the wall, and sand them smooth.

SAFETY TIP

The Dangers of Lead Paint

Although lead-based paint was banned in 1978, it is still found in more than 50 million homes. Scraping or sanding this paint creates lead dust or fumes that you can ingest into your lungs. As lead accumulates in your body, it can cause brain damage, reduced intelligence, kidney disease, blood disorders, and behavior problems. Those most at risk are children under six, unborn babies, and pregnant women. Thus, if you suspect that your wall is covered with lead-based paint, hire a professional to prepare it. The money saved in doing it yourself is not worth the risk of exposure to lead.

Choosing Paint and Supplies

When ordering paint, you must make two basic decisions. The first relates to the level of gloss in the paint. The gloss in paint is a measure of the resins present, which bind the paint to the surface. Paint ranges from high-gloss to flat. Higher-gloss paints are shinier and more durable and moisture-resistant.

The other decision to make is between latex and oil-based paint. If you are as messy as I am, this is an easy decision. Latex paint is water soluble, which means that everything (except for clothing) can be cleaned with warm, soapy water. It also dries quickly, has excellent color retention, and is practically free of noxious odors and dangerous fumes. Latex can be used over wallboard, bare masonry, and flat oil-based paint. It does not adhere well to high-gloss, oil-based finishes because it does not combine chemically with the painted surface. To use latex over a high-gloss oil paint, prime the surface first.

Oil-based paints require turpentine or mineral spirits for cleaning. The paint chemically bonds with the surface it is covering. High-gloss, oil-based paints are therefore resistant to water. They provide an excellent finish for areas that will need frequent washing. Otherwise, oil-based paints provide few advantages.

Save on paint by measuring the room first. A general rule is that one gallon of paint covers about 400 square feet. Measure the length, width, and height of your room and discuss these dimensions with a knowledgeable sales clerk. Also request that the paint be thoroughly mixed before you bring it home. Try to purchase all the paint you need at one time. Purchasing more of the custom color later may lead to an imperfect match.

In addition to paint, you will need a roller, a roller pan, a roller extension for high walls and ceilings, and a two-inch brush for painting molding, windows, and trim. With paint brushes, you get what you pay for, so purchase a brush that is at least medium priced. Finally, buy masking tape to cover surfaces that you want to keep unpainted such as glass panes in a window.

<u>Tools to Have on Hand:</u> steel tape measure, roller and roller pan, roller extension (as needed), paint brushes, razor blades (as needed)

Painting Tips

Now that you are ready to paint, here are a few tips to make the job go more smoothly.

- Cover the floor and furniture with an old sheet, newspapers, or a plastic tarp and be sure to wear old clothes — paint, even latex, is not easily removed from clothing.

- Paint bare surfaces with a primer first. The primer seals and protects the wall surface. It also helps to bond the finish coat to your walls. When the primer dries, begin painting.

- Do not load the roller or brush with too much paint. If the paint drips, you have too much paint.

- It is not a good idea to paint over hard-to-remove wall stains like rust, lipstick, or crayon marks. Often such stains will bleed through the paint. Instead, wash away as much of the stain as possible. Then seal the stain with white shellac. When the shellac dries, you can paint over it with your finish coat.

- Wait for wall surfaces to become completely dry before applying a second coat. Follow the directions on the paint can.

- Once the job is completed, clean your roller and brushes thoroughly so that they can be used again. Although latex paint is water soluble, it is nearly impossible to clean once it is dry. If you fail to complete the job in one day, your roller and brush can be wrapped in plastic and placed in the freezer for overnight storage. This avoids the time-consuming cleaning process.

- If you get paint on the glass in a window, you can easily scrape it off with a razor blade. Be careful, however, not to cut yourself. It is a good idea to cover one edge of the blade with protective tape.

- For painting the bottom of a baseboard in a room with wall-to-wall carpeting, use a protective shield as you go. Firm cardboard or plywood is perfectly adequate, although an inexpensive device for this purpose can be purchased at the paint-supply or hardware store.

- If you are painting a masonry surface, check carefully at the paint store for the correct paint and the correct roller nap.

Protect carpeting with a stiff shield as you paint baseboards.

Stenciling

The concept of stenciling is uncomplicated: One applies color through a hole cut in a piece of stencil material, which is held against the surface being decorated. The cut-out image may be printed over and over again, as long as the stencil material holds up. One of the few limitations on the design is that, in order to keep the stencil stable, large areas must be broken into smaller segments separated by "bridges." The way in which a design is segmented gives it its distinctively stenciled look.

Supplies and Materials

The materials needed for stenciling are also simple: a flat sheet from which to cut the design, a cutting tool, color, and a color applicator.

The Stencil. Many craft and art supply stores carry a large line of ready-cut stencils. If you wish to create your own design, purchase polyester stencil sheets (Mylar), which may be cut with an inexpensive stencil cutting pen. These stencil sheets, whether ready-cut or homemade, are long-lasting and easy to clean for reuse.

Brushes. Stencil brushes come in a wide variety of sizes. The nature and size of the project will dictate the size brush you need. For stenciling large areas, large brushes (1 inch) give better, more even coverage. For narrow, dainty borders or designs with small figures, a brush ½ inch or smaller works best. Stencil brushes have blunt-cut bristles. You may find some have softer bristles than others. Experiment to discover which gives the best texture for the project you are planning.

Sponges. For some projects, instead of brushes you may wish to use sponges to achieve interesting textural effects. Cut new, inexpensive sponges (they will be soft when first removed from the package) to the desired size. To apply the paint, either blot or scrub it through the stencil opening.

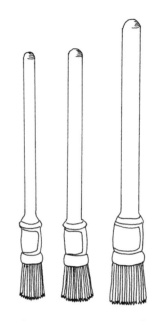

Brushes come in a variety of sizes.

Other Supplies. You will need a piece of glass, a paint tray, or some other nonabsorbent surface on which to pour a few drops of your paint. You will also need a piece of scrap paper (paper towel works well) on which to rub excess paint from the brush. If you plan to mix colors you will need several small containers.

Use a measuring tool, such as a yardstick or tape measure, to determine placement of the design. For marking very large spaces, you may need a chalk line to help keep lines straight. A level is useful for creating an exactly horizontal or vertical line on a wall that is not quite square.

Adhesive stencil spray is formulated to coat the back of the stencil for a temporary hold. It's very useful when stenciling walls, especially for large stencils. If you are stenciling on a painted surface, be sure it is completely dry, or the adhesive may pull up the paint.

Choosing Paint

A wide variety of colors and many kinds of paint may be used for stenciling. Most paints sold specifically for stenciling walls are acrylic. Because acrylic paint is water-based, it's easy to remove if a mistake is made. You may even use crayons, pastels, or marking pens, although with these you must be careful to avoid getting a darker-colored ridge around the outside of the stencil pattern. Some are also difficult to clean away if mistakes are made.

Placing the Design

In older houses, your ceiling line is unlikely to be straight. Before applying a stenciled border, place a level in several spots along the wall where it meets the ceiling. Small variations off level won't be noticeable, but if the ceiling is very uneven, use a level as a guide to draw a straight line.

Designs with a large repeat need more careful planning than small running designs. For a large repeating motif, mark the center of the wall, and then measure backwards from the design to find where to place the first print. For small running designs, you should be able to lay one design against the other all the way around the room, making the turns at the corners as smoothly and inconspicuously as possible.

Be sure to mix enough color to complete the project; it's hard to duplicate hand-mixed shades.

Applying Paint

The most common mistake beginning stencilers make is to apply too much paint. The result is smeared and dripping paint, soggy stencils, and discouraged artists. Remember, a couple of tablespoons of paint is enough to stencil a border for an entire room, so very little is needed for each print. Here's how to proceed:

1. Use tape or spray adhesive to position your stencil where you wish to print. Dribble a small amount of paint on your paint tray.

2. Dab the stencil brush into the paint in a circular motion to take up a small amount. On a piece of scrap paper, blot this little bit of paint out of the brush until only a faint shade shows.

3. Holding the brush upright, apply the paint through the stencil in a circular, scrubbing motion, as though you were a child scribbling on a piece of paper. It is usually best to work from the edge of the stencil toward the center of the area being printed. Remove the stencil. If your print smears or runs in any way, either you have used too much paint, the paint is too runny, or the back of your stencil is dirty.

Stenciling Tips

• When it is time to change colors, clean your brush well and allow it to dry completely before attempting to print with the next color. Wet brushes are likely to result in blurred or different colored prints.

• Between prints, gently clean the back of your stencil with a piece of soft cloth or tissue.

• If the project is complete and dry before a mistake is discovered, sand lightly to remove the error, reapply enough background color to cover the area completely, and restencil.

• On rough walls, dark lines may appear on the raised irregularities. To avoid this, use even less paint than usual and apply several coats until the desired color is achieved. (Leave the stencil taped or affixed to the wall while each coat dries; it's almost impossible to line the stencil up in the same place twice.)

• When you are finished with your stencils, clean them thoroughly and allow them to dry completely before storing flat.

Step 1: Dribble a small amount of paint on a tray.

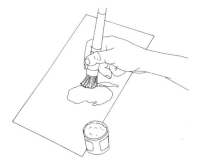

Step 2: Blot excess paint from brush onto scrap paper.

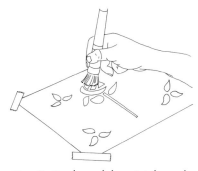

Step 3: Scrub or dab paint through stencil openings.

Working with Wallpaper

You can save lots of money by wallpapering a room by yourself. The work, though tricky at first, can be quite easily mastered.

Choosing Paper

With the walls prepared as they would be for painting, you are now ready to purchase the wallpaper. You will need to measure the wall area to be covered so that you can order the correct amount of paper. Bring the dimensions of the room to the store and the salesperson will be able to estimate the number of rolls required to complete the job. You may also find a chart in the back of a wallpaper book to help estimate the number of rolls needed. It is a good idea to bring home two additional rolls beyond the estimate so that you don't run out. Most stores will allow you to return unused paper.

The two most common wallpapers are vinyl and vinyl-coated papers. Vinyl papers contain a layer of solid vinyl that is bonded to the paper. They are long-lasting, strong papers that resist moisture and grease and can be washed with heavy-duty cleaners. As a result, they work well in high-traffic areas such as bathrooms, kitchens, and children's rooms.

Vinyl-coated papers contain vinyl coatings of varying thicknesses. They are usually prepasted, which means that the glue that enables them to adhere to the wall comes on the back of the paper. Vinyl-coated papers are not grease resistant, but they can be washed with mild soap and water. The quality of these papers varies greatly, so you will need to discuss the issues of price and quality with a knowledgeable salesperson.

A specialty wallpaper such as cork, linen, string, or grass cloth has its own set of instructions for hanging, as well as its own strengths and weaknesses regarding strength and durability. Again, you will need to discuss all these issues with a knowledgeable salesperson. My best advice for those papering for the first time is to keep the pattern simple. It is much easier to match along the wall.

Purchasing Equipment

While at the paper store, you will need to buy several pieces of equipment. To guide the placement of the first strip of paper, you will need a plumb line (a length of string that is weighted at the end) and colored chalk. A good purchase would be a chalk line. This is a spool of string enclosed in a chalk-filled dispenser. When the string is pulled out of the spool, it is covered with chalk. You will also need large, sharp scissors, a trimming knife with extra razor blades, a smoothing brush or large sponge, and a tape measure.

For paper that is not prepasted, wallpaper paste and a paste bucket and brush are necessary. For prepasted paper, you will need a water tray. It is also handy to have a large working table for cutting and pasting, and clean rags to remove excess paste.

<u>Tools to Have on Hand:</u> steel tape measure, plumb line, colored chalk, chalk line, scissors, trimming knife, smoothing brush or sponge, paste bucket (as needed), large brush (as needed), water tray (as needed)

Preparing Walls for Papering

<u>Tools to Have on Hand:</u> straight-slot or Phillips strewdriver (as needed), putty knife (as needed), wallpaper steamer (as needed), large paint brush

Prepare the walls as you would for painting. All cracks, holes, and bumps, both large and small, must be repaired. You also need to clean the walls thoroughly and remove all light switch and outlet covers. It is not a good idea to paper over vinyl or metallic foil, though you can paper over other wallpapers if they are in good condition.

If you are papering over old wallpaper, remove all loose wallpaper with a scraper. If there are large sections of loose paper or if you discover several layers of paper, it is best to remove all the old paper. For small areas, use a chemical solution to remove the old paper. For large areas, rent a wallpaper steamer.

When papering new plaster or sheetrock walls, two further steps are strongly recommended. First, apply a coat of flat primer-sealer to the walls, and then size them. You can purchase sizing powder from the hardware store. Mix it with water according to the directions on the can and brush or roll it on the walls. Allow it to dry overnight.

SAFETY TIP

Steamer Safety

Be careful when using these steamers. The steam that flows out is as hot as boiling water. Wear protective goggles and gloves, long pants, long sleeves, and shoes that completely cover your feet.

Removing Old Wallpaper

Removing wallpaper is a messy job. The trick is to soften the glue on the back side of the paper so that the paper can be scraped off.

<u>Tools to Have on Hand:</u> sponge, bucket, paint scraper (6-inch width), steamer (as needed), medium sandpaper, goggles and gloves (as needed)

Begin with a sponge, a pail of hot water, and a six-inch-wide scraper.

1. Use the sponge to thoroughly soak the old paper. If the glue has softened, the paper will slide along the wall.

2. Remove loosened sections of the paper with the scraper.

3. If the paper resists your scraper, try soaking it more. You can also purchase and add to the water wallpaper-removal products that help to soften the glue.

4. If nothing works, rent a wallpaper steamer and steam off the paper. Steamers are often necessary when walls are covered with several layers of paper.

5. Once you have succeeded in removing the old paper, you can use medium-grade sandpaper to sand off the remaining scraps of paper.

6. Before hanging new wallpaper, wash the wall with a household cleaner to remove any glue residue that remains.

SAFETY TIP

Caution with Chemical Strippers

Be careful when using chemical strippers to remove paper. Some are quite harsh and can burn your skin. Protect your hands and eyes with goggles and gloves when applying them and make sure the room is well ventilated.

Hanging Paper

<u>Tools to Have on Hand:</u> thumb tacks, scissors, plumb line, water tray (for prepasted papers), flat table (for unpasted papers), wallpaper paste (for unpasted papers), wallpaper brush (for unpasted papers), pail, wallpaper smoothing brush or large sponge, seam roller

1. Cut paper strips about 4 to 6 inches longer than the length of the wall. The extra amount can vary widely depending on the pattern selected. This overlap is necessary for proper matching. If you are cutting the paper by yourself, use a few thumb tacks at the top to hold the piece in place before cutting.

2. It's critical that you hang the first strip of paper perfectly straight. This is a problem because few walls are square. Here is where you use a plumb line. Put a piece of chalk at the end of the line, so you will be able to mark on the wall where the line has fallen. It is best to start alongside a door.

3. Measure the width of the paper. Then measure from the top of the door and mark the wall at a distance equal to the paper's width less one inch.

4. Attach your plumb line at the top of the wall where you marked it. Let it drop and when it stops moving, mark the spot where it stays. This will ensure a straight line.

5. Take your chalk line and hold it or attach it both at the top of the plumb line and at the spot where it landed. Pull the chalk line tight and snap it. This will leave a straight chalk line on the wall to use as a guideline for the first piece of paper.

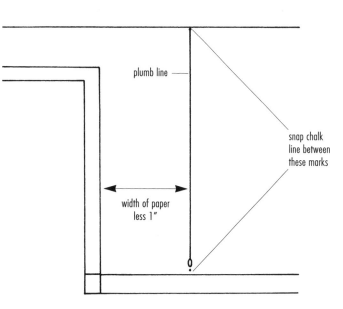

plumb line —

snap chalk line between these marks

width of paper less 1"

Snap a chalk line for the first strip at a point 1" narrower than the width of the paper.

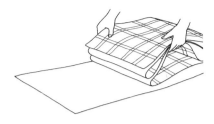

Step 6: Fold glued paper accordian style, glued sides together.

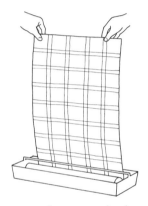

Step 7: Roll paper up backwards, and place in lukewarm water tray.

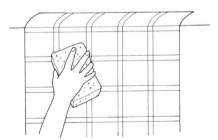

Step 9: Place top edge just above ceiling level. Use a sweeping motion to smooth from top to bottom with a large sponge or smoothing brush.

6. ***For paper requiring paste,*** place the cut paper on a table, pattern side down. Apply the paste generously with a brush. It is important to spread it evenly throughout and to make sure that the edges receive extra paste. Fold the paper, glued sides facing, accordian style, to make it easier to handle.

7. ***For prepasted paper,*** you will need to roll the paper up backwards, so that the glued side is facing out when placed in the lukewarm water tray. When you roll it up backwards, you will start with the bottom of the piece in order to have the top of the wallpaper pull out of the tray first. Immerse the roll in the tray and hold it so that it does not unravel for the length of time specified on the instructions that come with the paper. The paper is now ready to hang.

8. Place the water tray below the area where you are working and pull the paper up slowly, letting the excess water run off, ***or*** carry folded prepasted paper to the wall and lightly place top edge at ceiling level. Lightly press the paper onto the wall at the ceiling joint and in alignment with the plumb line. Make sure to leave a 2- to 3-inch overlap at the ceiling joint. Now align the lower portion with the baseboard and plumb line.

9. When the entire strip is placed properly on the wall, smooth from top to bottom several times with the smoothing brush or a large, wet sponge. Smooth from the center outward to the seams. Use a sweeping motion to prevent stretching.

10. Trim the paper at the ceiling joint, baseboard, and along the door frame. Remember that you established the plumb line 1 inch narrower than the width of the wallpaper. This was done because door frames are never quite straight. The trimming can be done in two ways. The first way is to create a crease in the paper by pushing it into the joint and then running a trimming knife along the crease. Some prefer, however, to pull the paper away from the wall after making the crease and then trim it with large, sharp scissors. If you do not use sharp scissors, the wallpaper will tear. When the trimming is finished, wipe away any excess paste with a clean sponge, continuously rinsing it in clean water. Now you are ready to hang the second strip.

11. Hang the second strip exactly the same way, using the first strip as the guiding line. The key problem is to match them properly. When cutting the paper, match at eye level and allow extra paper at the top and bottom. When applying the paper to the wall, you can either make a butt seam by bringing the two edges of the paper together with no overlap or create a ¹⁄₁₆-inch overlap. The first method is preferred because it is neater, but be aware that the paper tends to shrink as it dries and may therefore create thin gaps between the edges that are obvious. In both cases, you must be careful to match the pattern as closely as possible. If you have cut the strip long enough, you will have enough leeway to slide the strip up or down the wall until it matches. When there is a horizontal pattern such as dots, take a level and align the pattern on the first piece of paper to the pattern on the second piece (see drawing at right). If the bubble in the level is between the two vertical lines, you will know that the pattern does not go uphill or downhill. Be sure that you press along each seam with either a seam roller or a firm fingernail.

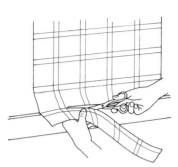

Step 10: Use the dull edge of your scissors to make a crease along the ceiling edge, then pull paper back to trim with sharp scissors. Gently press paper back into place.

Unglued Edges
Wallpaper may become unglued along the edges. If this happens, carefully lift the paper away from the wall and apply a seam repair adhesive to the back of the paper with a small artist's brush. Push the paper back into place and wipe the newly glued area clean with a damp sponge. You can purchase the seam repair adhesive at any wallpapering store.

Smoothing Out Bubbles
If a large bubble appears, peel the paper back off the wall to the bubble and smooth it out by brushing the bubble toward the seams. Next, move the paper slowly back onto the wall, smoothing as you go. If you end up with a bubble and the paper has started to dry, take the point of your razor's edge or utility knife or trimming knife and poke a hole in it, then smooth it out from the outside toward the hole.

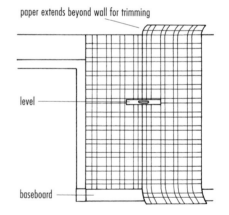

paper extends beyond wall for trimming

level

baseboard

Step 11: Be sure to leave excess paper at top and bottom to allow for the match.

Papering Corners

As you proceed along the wall, you will inevitably encounter a corner. It is tempting to round the corner, but corners are often not straight. A better strategy is to trim the excess paper at the corner leaving a one-inch overlap into the next wall and begin the next wall with a plumb line.

Papering around Windows

Hanging wallpaper around windows can be a problem. I prefer to do it without making extra cuts. Start the process as if the window were not there.

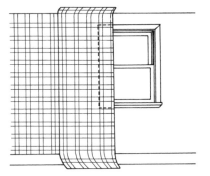

Hang the paper over the window as though it weren't there, then crease the paper where it should be trimmed, taking special care to mark the corners. When trimming, cut first into the corners, cutting at an angle.

1. Align the paper with the strip beside it and place it two inches above the ceiling joint. Attach the paper with your smoothing brush.

2. When you reach the window, make a crease along the entire window frame. Take special care to mark the corners. Trim away the paper that would otherwise cover over the window, cutting first at angles toward the corner marks and checking the vertical and horizontal marks once again (see drawing at left).

3. When the paper is glued into place, be sure to go over all the wallpaper with a clean, wet sponge in order to remove any excess paste.

Covering Outlets

1. Cover each outlet with a piece of masking tape so that water does not seep into the outlet.

2. Paper over the outlet as if it weren't there.

3. Poke a small hole in the paper as you go over the outlet so that you can find it later.

4. Turn off the electricity before trimming. After the paper is dry, trim the paper away from each outlet, taking care not to trim outside the area that will be covered by the switch or outlet cover.

5. Replace switch and outlet covers.

Covering Light Switches

A decorative touch to wallpapering is covering the switch plates.

1. Take a dry scrap piece of wallpaper and match it to the paper on the wall around the outlet. Place the switch plate under the matched paper.

2. Fold one side of the paper over the cover to make sure it still matches the pattern on the wall. Hold it tightly in place. Flip the switch plate over and scotch tape the paper to the backside of the plate.

3. Proceed this way for the opposite side. (You will have to cut the paper back on the inside of the plate so you can tape it to the plastic.)

4. In order to cut the corners on the other two sides you will need to make a cut and then fold.

5. After the cuts, fold the corners in toward the center, and tape them to the switch plate. This makes a clean corner.

6. To cut around the two plugs or a switch, take a sharp razor blade and follow the outline of the holes from the backside. If you only have scissors, trace the plug or switch holes, take the paper off and cut them out. Put the paper back on and tape it.

SAFETY TIP

Turn Off the Power

When papering around switches and outlets, turn off the power to avoid electrical shock. Wet wallpaper will conduct electricity. You need to be especially careful when working with foil paper.

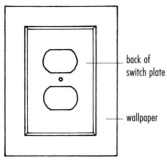
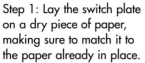

Step 1: Lay the switch plate on a dry piece of paper, making sure to match it to the paper already in place.

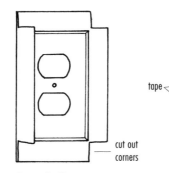

Step 4: Cut out the corners.

Step 5: Fold in the corners, and tape the paper in place.

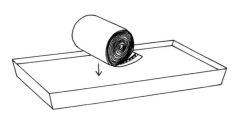

Step 3: Reroll the border paper and place it in a water tray.

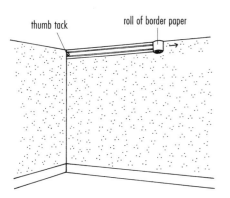

thumb tack   roll of border paper

Step 4: Tack the border paper at one corner, then roll it out into place.

Hiding Uneven Trimming

When the wall is fully covered with paper, stand back and admire your work. If your trimming hand was a little unsteady at times like mine, there is one additional step you can take to hide any unevenness that exists along the top edge.

1. Purchase a roll of border paper. Border paper is ordered in linear feet and usually comes in 5-yard rolls. This border paper is hung horizontally just below the ceiling joint. To hang border paper, you must use a vinyl-to-vinyl border adhesive or you will pay later, even if it says "prepasted."

2. Measure a piece of border paper a few inches larger than the length of the entire circumference of the room you are papering.

3. Take the whole roll of border paper and reroll it backwards. Place it in the water tray, or paste.

4. When hanging the border by yourself, place a few thumb tacks at the beginning in order to hold it as you move along the wall. It is helpful to have two or three stepstools set up ahead of time to jump onto as you go around the room.

5. When rounding the corners with the border, do not cut the paper completely. If the walls are not square, make a slit in the top a few inches down and overlap the paper in order for it to lie flat in the corner.

6. Make sure to clean your equipment thoroughly and save any unused wallpaper for patching later or for school and craft projects. That should complete your project.

Patching Damaged Paper

A small section of wallpaper may become damaged. Cut out a patch of new wallpaper that is big enough to cover the damaged area, being sure to match patterns. Use a razor blade to cut through the old paper and remove it. Glue on the new paper and wipe the new paper with a damp sponge.

Wallpapering the Bathroom

The key factor in wallpapering a bathroom is humidity. Some bathrooms never fully dry out. With this in mind, your best bet is to go with prepasted vinyls, either cloth- or paper-backed, because they are more water resistant. You should also make sure that they come with a moisture-resistant adhesive.

The main reason for recommending prepasted paper is convenience. Bathrooms are usually small rooms, which means that the large worktable necessary for spreading paste to paper would not fit well. In addition, bathtubs provide an excellent source of water for prepasted paper.

Placing new paper over old paper is not a good idea in the bathroom. Because of the moisture problem, one should always be suspicious of the condition of the old paper. This is especially true if you plan to hang vinyl paper. Because the vinyl paper will create an airtight seal over the old paper, mildew will have an ideal environment to grow in the old paste.

From a decorative perspective, large patterns get interrupted in small bathrooms by corners and fixtures. This makes it difficult for the eye to understand what the paper is all about. Also, be aware that the walls are often not perfectly straight and square. This creates problems for stripes and plaids with evenly spaced lines. They can become distorted. Your best bet is to choose small- to medium-sized prints with frequent repetitions.

MAKING IT LAST

Cleaning Wallpaper

Wallpaper in high-traffic areas often becomes spotted from dirty hand marks. If the room accumulates large amounts of smoke from fireplaces, wood stoves, or cigarettes, it is likely to acquire a grayish-black tinge.

You can wash dirt and stains from washable or vinyl wallpaper by using a solution of mild soap and water. It is not a good idea to use strong chemical cleaners.

Nonwashable paper presents more of a problem. Gum erasers and some commercial spot removers will lighten the stain. Real problem stains will have to be patched. That is why it is always a good idea to keep scrap pieces of wallpaper that remain after you do the initial hanging.

Chapter Seven

Floors

Floors

AT A GLANCE

- ceramic tile
- vinyl flooring
- wood floors
- carpet

and more

The Structure of Floors

A well-maintained floor does a lot to enhance a room, while a scratched wood finish or stained carpet can be an eyesore. Whether you plan to refinish a wood floor or install ceramic tile, it's important to understand floor construction.

Most home floors have three layers — a subfloor that is attached to the floor joists, an underlayment that is laid over the subfloor, and the finished flooring (see drawing below). It helps to have the subfloor as solid as possible. Concrete is the best surface. A wood subfloor is also fine, but you should cover it with an underlayment of plywood. Unpadded linoleum works well, too, provided it is glued firmly in place. If you want to add new flooring to a room, you can often put it directly over the old flooring if the latter is in good shape. The old flooring or subfloor must be free of dirt because dirt weakens the adhesive bond. It is also necessary to fill in all cracks and holes and to nail down loose boards.

It is easier and faster to keep the old flooring, but this does add height to the new floor, which may pose problems. If the old flooring has badly deteriorated, it must be removed or a new underlayment must be placed over it. Whether or not you remove the old flooring, you will need to add a new underlayment. The two most common types of underlayment are plywood and hardboard, which come in 4 x 4 and 4 x 8 foot sheets. The secret to a good job is to arrange the wood sheets in a staggered pattern so that the joints of adjacent sheets are not perfectly aligned. It's a good

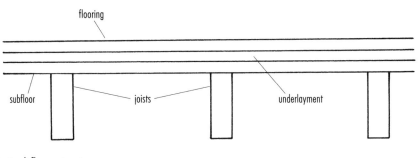

Typical floor structure

idea to create a $\frac{1}{32}$- to $\frac{1}{8}$-inch crack between each sheet to allow for expansion. Use fourpenny, resin-coated nails to fasten the sheets to the subfloor. Space the nails about six inches apart throughout the entire surface.

Vinyl Flooring

Vinyl flooring is made of polyvinyl chloride and comes in both tile and sheet forms. This flooring is also called resilient flooring because of its softness underfoot. It is sometimes confused with linoleum, a product that is no longer manufactured in the United States. Although some vinyl floors look like the old linoleum, they are much improved in terms of durability and resistance to wear.

In its sheet form, this flooring comes in three types. Sheet vinyl is solid vinyl. It is durable, and because it is made from pure vinyl it tends to be the most expensive type. Unfortunately, it is difficult to lay. Cushioned sheet vinyl comes with foam backing. There are several grades of this vinyl available, varying in durability and resistance to wear. Roto sheet vinyl is made from a cellulose felt or mineral fiber base with a thin coat of vinyl for its cover. It is easy to lay and relatively inexpensive; however, it tends to be less durable than the other types.

Solid vinyl tiles have the same characteristics and composition as sheet vinyl. Vinyl asbestos tile is the most popular and is durable, resistant to wear, and easy to install if you select the adhesive-backed variety.

The technological advances in these floorings have been generally matched with more generous warranties. Many products are guaranteed against mildew. The warranties on performance and durability range from five to ten years for sheet vinyl and one to five years for tile. All warranties are contingent on proper installation and some require professional installation. Few warranties are transferable to a new owner.

Problems with Flooring

PROBLEM	CAUSE	REMEDY	PAGE
Holes in vinyl flooring		Patch hole	154
Cracked ceramic tile		Use tile repair kit to repair crack	158
		Replace tile	158
Crack in grout		Fill crack with silicone tile and tub caulk	158
		Regrout	158
Mold, mildew, or dirt on tile		Clean tile	159
Worn, scratched, or stained finish on wood floor		Refinish wood floor	160–161
Squeaky floors	Boards rubbing together or against nail	Pound in loose nails; insert wooden shim in gap between joists and subflooring	159
		Consult building contractor	
Dirt, spills, or stains on carpet		Clean carpet	164–165
		Steam clean carpet	165

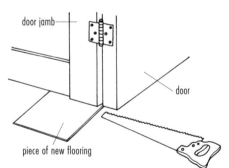

door jamb

door

piece of new flooring

Step 3: You may need to trim the door jamb in order to fit in the new piece of flooring.

Laying Vinyl Flooring

<u>Tools to Have on Hand:</u> hammer (as needed), crosscut or power saw (as needed), pry bar (as needed), utility knife, notched trowel, metal straightedge

1. Prepare the subfloor (see page 150).

2. Gently pry up the baseboard in such a way that you do not damage it.

3. Try sliding a piece of the new flooring under the door jamb. If it doesn't fit, you will need to trim the door jamb so that the new flooring will fit under it.

4. Cut and trim the vinyl sheets to fit your floor. The initial cut should leave each sheet with an additional 3 inches on all sides. The overlap will curl up along each wall when the sheet is laid out on the floor. It is a good idea to put a piece of plywood under the vinyl when cutting so that you do not damage the floor underneath.

5.   To trim the overlap, create a crease along the wall. Using a sharp utility knife and a straightedge for a guide, cut the vinyl sheet along the crease. When trimming, leave a very small gap (about ⅛ inch) between the flooring and the wall to allow for expansion.

6.   You are now ready to glue the vinyl sheets to the subfloor. For this task you will need to purchase a notched trowel to apply the adhesive. Roll up one-half of your fitted sheet and apply the glue according to the manufacturer's directions. Leave the edge(s) that will be along the seam unglued.

7.   Press the sheet into place and make sure that the flooring fits evenly up to the edge of the wall. Repeat this process for the other half of the sheet.

8.   Once the flooring is glued in place, take a 2 x 4 about a yard in length and move it up and down the entire floor while applying downward pressure. This will ensure that the vinyl is properly bonded to the sub-floor. You might want to place a towel underneath the 2 x 4 to protect your new flooring.

9.   If your floor is wider than the vinyl sheet, it will be necessary to align two sheets together by creating a seam. As you glue the first sheet to the subfloor, leave several inches of space where the seam will be located without glue. Slide the new sheet under the one you have just glued and match the patterns exactly. Place a metal straightedge along the edge of the top sheet. Using the straightedge as a guide, cut the bottom sheet with a sharp utility knife. Fold back the top sheet, remove the bottom strip, apply glue to the subfloor, and press the two sheets into place.

10.   Wash any excess glue from your new flooring with warm water.

11.   When reattaching the baseboard, it is a good idea to leave a small space between it and the floor to allow the vinyl to expand and contract according to changes in the humidity in your room.

12.   Follow the manufacturer's instructions regarding drying time for the glue, and save the excess vinyl for later repairs.

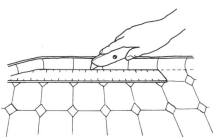

Step 5: Trim the overlap with a sharp utility knife and a straightedge for a guide.

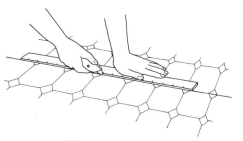

Step 9: Align pattern carefully where two sheets create a seam.

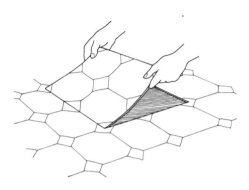

Use a straightedge to cut out the damaged area, then replace it with a clean new piece.

Repairing Vinyl Flooring

Over time, vinyl flooring can become damaged with holes, tears, and blisters. Large holes that develop need to be patched.

<u>Tools to Have on Hand:</u> metal straightedge, utility knife, putty knife (as needed), iron (as needed)

1. Select a replacement patch that closely matches the pattern of the damaged piece.

2. Take a pencil and draw a square around the damaged area.

3. Using a straightedge to guide you, cut along the line with a sharp utility knife.

4. ***If the vinyl is not glued to the subfloor,*** lift out the damaged section, spread glue onto the subfloor, and press the patch into place. Wipe off any excess glue that may have oozed around the edges and weight down the patch evenly for at least 24 hours.

5. ***If the vinyl is glued down,*** you can often peel it up by shoving a putty knife underneath the flooring. If that doesn't work, use an iron to weaken the glue. Place the iron on a damp cloth rather than placing it directly on the vinyl. Lift out the vinyl, spread glue on the subfloor, and press the patch into place.

6. ***For vinyl that is torn,*** lift the torn section, spread new glue, and press the torn section back into place. Cover the damaged area with a weighted board for a minimum of 24 hours.

7. ***For a blister,*** flatten it by cutting through its center. You now have a tear, which can be fixed as outlined above.

Laying Ceramic Tile

Ceramic tile is attractive, moisture resistant, tough, and easily cleaned. It makes an excellent floor cover for bathrooms and kitchens. Although laying the floor yourself is time consuming, you will save lots of money.

The first step is to purchase the tile. Tile comes in many different styles, colors, and sizes. The most common sizes are 4-, 6-, 8-, and 12-inch squares. The larger the tile, the easier the installation; but you will have to live with it, so choose what looks best.

Tile also comes in two surfaces. Unglazed tile is hardened clay with the color and texture of natural clay. Glazed tile has a smooth, shiny coating. It is easier to clean but slippery when wet, which means it may not be the best choice for your bathroom. When purchasing tile, give the dimensions of your room to the salesperson, who will be able to determine the amount you need. Remember to purchase extra tile for later repairs and in case you end up breaking a few.

While at the building-supply store, you will need to purchase the following materials: plastic spacers, glue, and grout. The salesperson will be able to recommend the best brands of these products. Ask if it is possible to rent a wet saw — the tool used to cut tile. It is an expensive tool to buy. In addition to the wet saw, you will need tile-cutting pliers, a notched spreader, a plastic spreader for the grout, rubber gloves, a straightedge, and a chalk line.

Laying the Tile

There are many different approaches to laying tile. My favorite is to begin by dividing the room into four equal sections.

<u>Tools to Have on Hand:</u> chalk line, wet saw (rent if possible), tile-cutting pliers, notched spreader, plastic spreader, level (as needed)

1. Find the midpoint for each wall and mark off the room into four quadrants using a chalk line (see page 141).

2. Begin laying the tile, without gluing it, at the midpoint of the room (the point where the lines intersect) and work within one quadrant from the midpoint to the outer walls.

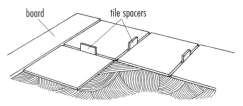

board   tile spacers

Align tiles against a board, and place tile spacers between the pieces as you lay them.

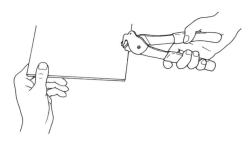

Use tile-cutting pliers to trim out small pieces in tile to fit around doors and pipes.

3. Place plastic spacers between each tile so that the amount of space between them is the same.

4. You may also want to use a board to make sure that the tiles are aligned in a straight line. Do this for all four sections of the room.

Although time consuming, there are two advantages to laying out all the tiles first before gluing them. If the space along the wall for the last tile is an inch or less, it will be very difficult to cut the tile without splitting it. You can correct this problem by moving the chalk line dividing the room three inches closer to the wall.

Cutting Tile

The other problem is cutting the tiles. This is the most difficult part of the project. The best way to cut floor tile is with a wet saw, which is an expensive tool. If all your tiles are laid out, you can mark the tiles that need to be cut and take them to a building supply store. If they have a wet saw, they will usually cut them all for free. If that doesn't work, ask the salesperson where you can rent such a saw. Make sure to wear safety glasses when using this saw to prevent chips from landing in your eyes.

To cut around a doorframe, pencil out the area on the tile that needs to be cut. Then take tile-cutting pliers and slowly chip away at the section to be removed. It is a good idea to wear safety goggles when cutting tile to prevent flying ceramic chips from getting in your eyes. For fitting around a pipe, plan to have the tile come up to the edge of the pipe. Mark the area along the edge to be removed with a pencil and then chip away small bits of tile at a time with the tile-cutting pliers (see drawing at left).

Gluing Tile

1. When you are ready to glue the tile, pick up the tile in one quadrant of the room.

2. Apply glue to the subfloor with a notched spreader in an area of about one square yard.

3. Starting at the midpoint of the room, press the tile into the adhesive and insert the spacers. You must be careful to keep the tiles in a straight row and at the same height.

4. After completing each square-yard section, balance a 2 x 4 on the tiles to check for height. Push down any tiles that are raised too high. You can also use a level for this task.

5. Check the manufacturer's instructions on the adhesive for drying time. Drying time is usually a minimum of 24 hours.

6. Once the adhesive has thoroughly dried, the last step is to fill the cracks with grout. Pour a generous amount of grout onto the tiles and spread it with a special plastic spreader. Make sure to work it into all the seams.

7. Remove the excess grout as you go and then clean the entire surface with a damp sponge. Thoroughly clean the tiles again the next day with the same damp sponge.

8. Grout creates a stronger bond if it is kept damp for two or three days. In this regard, it helps to cover the floor with plastic while your tile is drying to seal in the moisture.

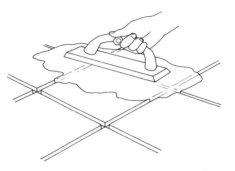

Step 6: Pour a generous amount of grout onto the tiles, and then spread it with a plastic spreader, working the grout into all seams.

Repairing Tile

If the problem is a small crack, it can easily be fixed with a ceramic tile repair kit, which you can buy at a hardware store. Read the directions to make sure the kit contains the right mix of paints to match the color of your tile. Using these same directions, mix the epoxy to fill in the cracks.

If the tile must be removed, your project becomes more difficult because the tile is firmly glued to the subfloor.

<u>Tools to Have on Hand</u>: straight-slot screwdriver (as needed), ice pick (as needed), hair dryer or iron (as needed), pry bar (as needed), putty knife

1. Begin by removing the grout with a screwdriver or ice pick. Be careful not to cut yourself or damage adjacent tiles as you work.

2. Soften the glue with heat. You can do this with your hair dryer or by working the tile with a medium-hot iron. Make sure to protect the tile with a damp cloth and be careful not to heat adjacent tiles.

3. After applying the heat, slip a putty knife under the tile and pry up. If that does not do the job, lift up with a pry bar. It is a good idea to use a 2 x 4 for leverage and to protect the adjacent tile.

4. Once the tile is removed, use a putty knife to scrape away as much of the old glue as possible.

5. Apply a new coat of adhesive and insert a new tile that matches your pattern. If the new tile is a little too large, you can solve the problem by sanding the edges. Cover the new tile with a board and a light weight while the glue dries. If you are gluing the new tile to a vertical wall, hold the new tile in place with strips of masking tape.

6. Complete the project by applying grout to the seams after the specified drying time is over.

Repairing Cracks in Grout

Do not allow cracks between ceramic tiles to go unfixed. If you do, water will enter into the cracks and loosen the surrounding tile or damage the wallboard to which the tile is attached.

<u>Tool to Have on Hand</u>: awl

Use an awl to clean out the old grout along the crack and then fill the crack with silicone tile and tub caulk. If the cracks between the tiles are extensive, it will be necessary to regrout the entire tile area.

Cleaning Tile

<u>Tools to Have on Hand:</u> stiff brush, rubber gloves

To remove mold, mildew, and dirt from ceramic tile, mix nine parts water to one part each of chlorine bleach and dishwashing detergent. Scrub the grout with a stiff brush and use rubber gloves to protect your hands.

Repairing Squeaky Floors

Squeaky floors result from two boards rubbing against each other or a board moving against a nail. These squeaks are a common problem because floors frequently move as they expand, contract, or flex under the weight of people in the room. This movement causes them to press against each other.

If you have a basement with exposed floor joists, the problem can probably be fixed quite easily.

<u>Tools to Have on Hand:</u> hammer, crosscut saw (as needed)

1. Begin by examining the floor from above for any loose nails. Pound them in.

2. Locate the squeak. Have a friend walk over your floor while you listen in the basement. Mark the spot where you hear the noise and then check for gaps between the floor joists and subflooring.

3. If you find a small gap, hammer a wedge-like wooden shim that is covered with glue into the gap.

4. For longer gaps, take a 2 x 4 about twice as long as the gap and glue the top edge against the subflooring. Force the 2 x 4 tightly against the subflooring, and nail the 2 x 4 to the floor joist.

If you find long gaps in one or more joists, you should consult a building contractor. It may be that you need additional support for your flooring system.

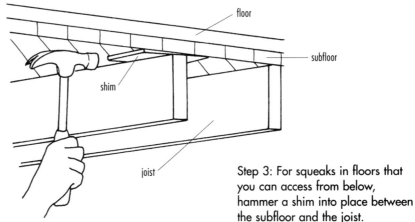

Step 3: For squeaks in floors that you can access from below, hammer a shim into place between the subfloor and the joist.

Refinishing Wood Floors

There is nothing prettier than a well-maintained wood floor. Over time, however, the finish on these floors wears off, and scratches, burns, and stains appear. Most wood floors can be refinished quite easily. I like to do mine every three or four years.

The key to the project is getting a new coat of polyurethane to adhere to the old finish. This is usually a simple process as long as the wood floor was not waxed. Older wood floors installed before 1970 were usually finished with a hard wax. These floors can be restored by being cleaned, rewaxed, and buffed. If this doesn't do the job, you will have to sand off the old finish to the bare wood and start over. That is not an easy project.

<u>Tools to Have on Hand:</u> sandpaper, buffer (optional), electric sander (optional), large paint brush

1. Assuming you have a newer floor that is free of wax, your first task is to remove all the furniture and lightly sand the floor to roughen the surface a little so that the new coat of polyurethane adheres to the old finish. This doesn't mean taking off the old finish, only gently sanding it.

Some people prefer to use a buffer or large electric sander to do this task. These machines are very powerful and difficult to handle.

Because any grit on the floor has the potential of becoming a scratch, you must make sure that the floor surface is clean and be careful not to take off more of the old coat than is necessary. If you decide to use one of these machines, make sure to get good instructions on its use from a knowledgeable salesperson at the rental equipment store.

2. The most difficult part of the job is to remove scratches, burns, or stains. Begin by hand-sanding the affected area with coarse sandpaper. If that seems to take forever, try a hand-held electric sander.

3. Once the affected area is repaired, you should apply a preliminary coat of polyurethane to that area to protect the wood. If the area had been stained, first restain the sanded area with a stain that is a little lighter than the original stain before applying polyurethane. The stain you apply to the sanded area will darken slightly with age.

Hard-to-Find Squeaks
For upstairs floors or basements where joists are covered, correcting squeaks may be more trouble than it's worth.

SAFETY TIP

Polyurethane Alert
Polyurethane contains chemical solvents, so wear a painting respirator if you are adversely affected by this floor finish and ventilate the room well while the polyurethane is drying.

4. When the light sanding is completed, sweep the floor thoroughly, and then damp-mop it. (Dampen your mop with mineral spirits or with a mixture of water and ¼ cup white vinegar to prevent stains.)

5. When the floor is thoroughly clean and dry, apply oil-based polyurethane. Apply it evenly with a large paint brush. Water-based polyurethane is easier to clean up, but it dries very quickly, so you have to work quickly and be careful not to leave ridges as you go.

6. For a long-lasting finish, apply three or four coats of polyurethane. Lightly sand the floor after each coat dries, and make sure that the floor is free of dust before applying the next coat.

Refinishing Painted Wood Floors

You have a different project on your hands if you want to remove paint from a wood floor and apply a clear finish.

<u>Tools to Have on Hand:</u> electric sander (as needed), drum sander (as needed), belt sander (as needed)

If the paint is thinly coated on the wood, you can use an electric sander. For a large floor, you will need to rent a drum sander (it looks like a large vacuum cleaner) and a smaller belt sander for the edge along the baseboards. Make sure you receive proper instructions for operating the drum sander from the rental company. These are powerful machines and can damage your floor if not used properly. Also make sure you wear a dust mask and ventilate the room you are working in because sanding will create a lot of dust.

For wood flooring with a heavy accumulation of paint, you will have to apply a paint remover first. This liquid is painted on with a brush. The remover softens the paint, which you can then remove with a scraper. This is a very messy and time-consuming process. After completing it, the floor will probably need to be sanded to remove any paint that remains. Remember that the imperfections that remain in the wood will be emphasized when you apply the clear finish.

SAFETY TIP

Paint Alert
• Paint removers are toxic substances. Read the safety precautions on the label before undertaking this rather nasty job.
• If you think your floor is covered with lead-based paint, hire a professional to remove it (see page 132 for dangers of lead paint).

Drum sander

Belt sander

Installing Carpet

Carpets offer an attractive and practical floor covering. You can install them yourself with only a few tools, but you need to be aware of two problems. First, carpets are heavy, so it helps to do this project with at least one friend and perhaps several. Second, without expensive tools it is difficult to stretch the carpet tightly to the wall. You can, however, achieve a good, though maybe not perfect, result on your own.

Tool to Have on Hand: steel tape measure, hammer, utility knife and razor blades, masonry nails (as needed), seaming iron (as needed), straightedge (as needed)

Carpets can be bonded to a subfloor with glue, double-sided tape, or tack strips. Glue is used most frequently for laying down commercial carpet and is not necessary for most residential situations. Double-sided tape often does not provide an adequate bond and is therefore not recommended. This leaves tack strips.

Tack strips are narrow wood slats with tacks sticking up from them. They need to be placed alongside each wall about ½ inch from the wall. If you have a wooden subfloor, it is easy to nail these strips into place. If you are working with a concrete subfloor, the job is more difficult. You can nail the strips into the concrete with masonry nails, or if that is too difficult, the strips can be glued in place.

For this project you will need, in addition to the carpeting, tack strips to fit the dimensions of your room, seam tape (and access to a seaming iron) if the room is wider than the carpet width, and a utility knife with plenty of razor blades. The first step is to obtain an accurate measurement of the room to be carpeted. This will require measurements from several places because the room may not be square. Once you have obtained the dimensions of your room, you will need to purchase enough carpet so that there is an overlap of 4 inches for each wall. Depending on the type of carpet you're installing and the subfloor, you may also need to purchase padding to go underneath the carpet. Ask a knowledgeable salesperson if this is necessary.

1. Before laying out the carpet, prepare the subfloor by getting rid of all dust, repairing any cracks, and securing loose tiles and/or floorboards.

2. Nail or glue the tack strips into place alongside each wall about ½ inch from the wall.

3. To lay out the carpet, start from the middle of the room and work toward each wall. Press the carpet against each wall and allow the carpet to settle for a few hours. This allows gravity to take care of some of the wrinkles and folds. To further straighten the carpet, raise one of the corners, stand on the subfloor, and gently kick the carpet.

4. Once in place, the carpet can now be cut. Be sure to leave 4 inches of overlap on each side for trimming. The best tool for cutting carpet is a utility knife. Make sure that the blade is sharp. Sharp blades make your cuts easier, cleaner, and safer.

5. If the width of the carpet is smaller than the width of the room, you will need to attach two pieces of carpet with seam tape. Plan to keep the seam away from high-traffic areas such as a doorway. Cut the seam tape the length of the seam you will be making.

6. With your two large pieces of carpet in their approximate places, it is important to align the carpet naps so that they are facing in the same direction. The nap consists of the fibers that make up the surface area of the carpet. The best way to determine whether the naps are aligned is to rub your hand along the carpet fibers. Rubbing in one direction will smooth out the fibers while rubbing in the other direction will raise them.

7. Once satisfied that the naps are facing the same way, fold back one carpet section and draw a line on the subfloor along the edge of the carpet that remains in place.

8. Fold back the other piece of carpet and place the seam tape on the subfloor with the line serving as the midpoint.

9. Now run the seaming iron across the tape to melt the glue. Place one section of the carpet firmly on the tape and lay the second carpet section as close to it as possible. Use your hands on both sides of the seam to press the two sections of carpet together as tightly as you can.

10. You now have the carpet in place with a 4-inch overlap along each wall. The next step is to trim the carpet. If you have baseboards, cut the carpet again so that the overlap is reduced to 1 inch. If you don't have baseboards, push the carpet firmly against the wall and trim as close to the edge as you can.

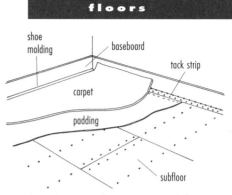

Step 2: Use tack strips around the entire perimeter of the room, about ½" from the wall.

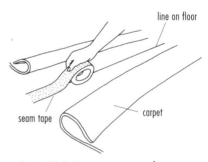

Steps 7–8: Run seam tape between pieces of carpet.

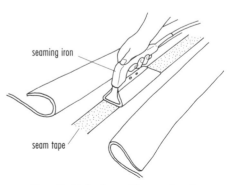

Step 9: Melt glue with seaming iron.

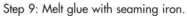

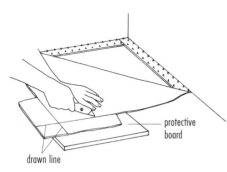

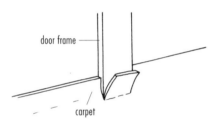

Step 11: To trim a corner, fold the carpet back toward you and use a protective board when you cut.

door frame

carpet

Step 12: Cut along both sides of the door frame, from the edge to the floor.

Carpet Remnants
Be sure to save any excess carpet. It comes in handy for carpet repair and for carpeting such places as closets.

11. *To trim a bunched-up corner,* fold the carpet back toward you. On the back side of the carpet, use a straightedge to draw two lines that continue the earlier cuts. Place a protective board between the folded carpet and the carpeted floor and cut along the lines with a sharp utility knife.

12. *To trim around a door frame,* cut along both sides of the frame, cutting from the edge of the overlap piece down toward the floor. Fold the carpet back and cut away the strip at the base of the door frame. Then create a crease at the door opening and cut along the crease. If the carpet ends there, it is a good idea to purchase a metal doorstrip to help hold the carpet firmly in place.

13. Secure the carpet by pushing the carpet edge into the tacks on the tack strips. If you have a baseboard, push the carpet into the tacks and then slip the excess carpet under the baseboard. If you don't have a baseboard, push the carpet edge as close to the wall as possible and then press down hard on the tacks. This should complete the project.

Patching Carpet
I first discovered how to solve a problem with our carpet the hard way.
<u>Tool to Have on Hand:</u> utility knife

When we became proud owners of a cat, we had no idea how to train it. A month later we had a very smelly carpet. Luckily, the problem was easily fixed. I cut out the section of damaged carpet with a sharp utility knife. From a piece of surplus carpet, I cut an identical replacement piece. If you do not have surplus carpet, cut your patch from carpet that is hidden from view, such as in a closet. Apply several strips of double-sided tape to secure the patch to the subfloor, although you can also use an appropriate glue that you buy at the carpet supply store. That should patch things up nicely.

Carpet Cleaning Tips
The quicker you deal with carpet stains, the better. Here are some tips:
• Try to determine the material from which your carpet was made, either by reading the product literature or the carpet label. Different carpet materials react differently to specific cleaning agents. You don't want to bleach your carpet or make the stain worse. If you cannot determine

the carpet material, test the cleaning solution you plan to use on a piece of scrap carpet or a piece that is hidden from general view. If the cleaning solution damages the carpet, choose a less potent cleaner.

- Never rub the carpet to get it clean because you will grind the stain into the carpet, which makes it worse. After applying the cleaning solution, use paper towels and blot the stain to lift it out.
- For surface stains, allow them to dry and then try clipping off the soiled surface with scissors.
- Store a number of cleaning agents in your kitchen so that they are there when you need them. Possible choices include general household cleaners, dry-cleaning fluid, ammonia, white vinegar, rubbing alcohol, and lemon juice. Never use ammonia on wool carpets and remember to always test a cleaning solution on a carpet scrap or hidden piece before using the solution to clean a stain.
- If you have Indian cotton rugs, antique rugs, needlepoint rugs, or hand-knitted carpets, it is best to leave the cleaning to a professional.
- As a preventive measure, you can treat your carpet with a chemical stain repellent. Such a treatment seals the carpet fibers and makes stain removal much simpler. Ask at your local carpet store for the proper protective solution to apply.
- Regular vacuuming will prevent dirt and stains from being ground in permanently.

Steam Cleaning

Once a year it is a good idea to steam clean your carpet. A steam cleaner forces a solution of cleaning detergent and hot water into your carpet and vacuums up the dirt and water. You can rent these easy-to-use machines from carpet dealers and many supermarkets.

Tools to Have on Hand: steam cleaner (rented), vacuum cleaner

1. Begin by thoroughly vacuuming the carpet to be cleaned.
2. It is often a good strategy when using a steam cleaner to move slowly across the carpet in one direction. After finishing the entire carpet, redo the carpet at right angles to your original path.
3. Allow the carpet about a day to dry before moving furniture back and permitting heavy foot traffic on the carpet.

SAFETY TIP

Carpet Vapors

Unfortunately, some new carpets emit volatile organic compounds (chemical vapors) into the air. These vapors are believed to cause respiratory problems and allergy-related headaches. Therefore, as a precaution, make sure that a newly carpeted room is properly ventilated for several days after installation.

MAKING IT LAST

Cleaning Compatibility

Some cleaning solutions can damage certain types of carpet fibers. Therefore it is important to follow the manufacturer's instructions when cleaning your carpet. If you do not have these instructions, ask about your carpet at a carpet supply store.

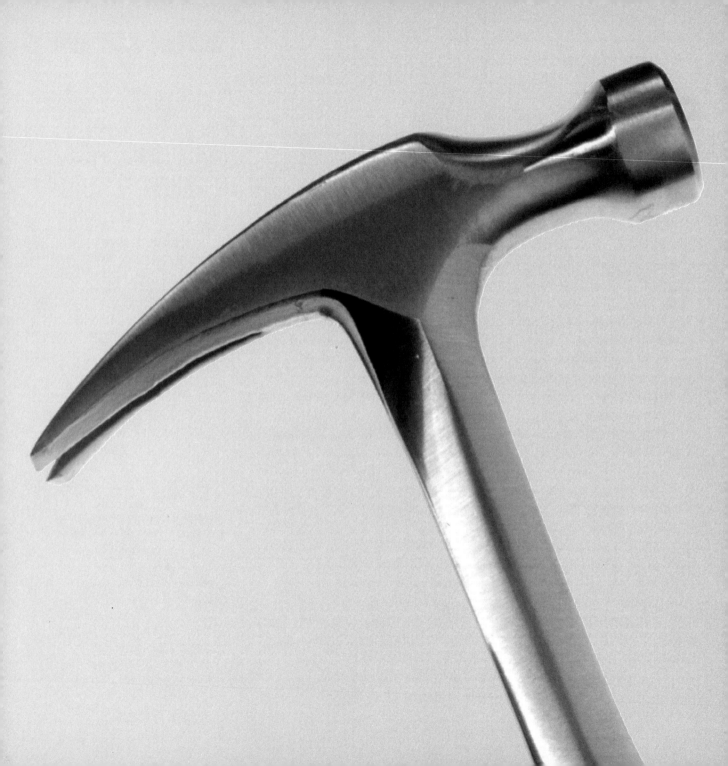

Chapter Eight

8

Furniture

AT A GLANCE

- scratches in wood
- stuck drawers
- upholstery stains
- sagging shelves

and more

Furniture

PROBLEM	CAUSE	REMEDY	PAGE
Water rings on furniture	Damp glass	Treat with polyurethane; apply mayonnaise, toothpaste, etc.	169
Scratches on furniture	Sharp/gritty object	Treat with furniture crayon, Old English Furniture Polish	169
Chair rungs/table legs come apart		Use Woodmate's Mr. Grip furniture repair kit	170
Wooden cabinet drawers stick	Nail in way	Remove nail	170
	Runners worn	Sand runners	171
Cabinet drawer sags		Turn bottom upside down	170
Cabinet comes apart at joints		Apply wood glue	171
Cabinet door won't latch	Problem with hinge	Tighten screw	172
Cabinet door sticks		Sand door	172
Stains on upholstery	Spills	Spot removal: blot with clean towel, send for brochure on spot removal	172
Sagging closet shelf	Overloaded, not properly supported	Install support board, turn shelf upside down	172–173

Furniture requires care and repair to keep it looking and functioning its best. With a little ingenuity you can fix those everyday annoyances like stubborn wooden drawers, loose cabinet latches, and scratches in wood furniture.

Removing Water Rings

When a damp glass is left on a piece of wood furniture, what often results is a white ring. This white ring is removable by applying mayonnaise to the affected area. The oil in the mayonnaise penetrates into the wood and returns it to its natural color. You may also use cooking oil for this task. Other applications include mixing butter and ashes, toothpaste, nondetergent ammonia, and a combination of baking soda and 4000 steel wool. Mr. Formby and Bri-wax are good commercial products for furniture doctoring.

Protecting Furniture

To prevent water rings, you can treat the wood surface of your furniture with polyurethane or another water-resistant coating.

<u>Tools to Have on Hand:</u> paint brush, fine sandpaper

The polyurethane is applied like paint or stain and can be purchased at the hardware or paint supply store. Two or three coats are usually required to provide adequate protection. A light sanding in between coats is recommended to get out bubbles and bumps. For antiques or other fine furniture, apply tung oil instead of polyurethane.

Removing Scratches

Several excellent products for removing scratches from furniture are available at the hardware store. Furniture crayons and Old English Furniture Polish are two products that work very well. Most of these products will not only help to hide the scratch but they also condition the wood.

Securing Chair Rungs and Table Legs

Several years ago my father refinished a beautiful Windsor chair for us. The problem now is that the rungs keep coming apart. I tried gluing them several times but that fix never lasts.

A friend recommended that I try Woodmate's Mr. Grip furniture repair kit. The kit contains several aluminum gripper strips with teeth.
<u>Tools to Have on Hand:</u> scissors

To fix a chair, you simply cut the strips to fit around the wooden peg at the end of the rung. You then firmly push the rung into place to tightly secure the joint. In addition to fixing chairs, the kit can be used to fix tables, stools, benches, brooms, wooden toys, and several other household items.

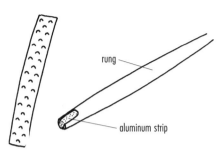

rung

aluminum strip

Woodmate's Mr. Grip furniture repair kit contains aluminum gripper strips to tighten chair rungs.

Unsticking Wooden Drawers

A common problem with wood cabinets is that over time the drawers begin to stick. There are several simple things you can do to remedy this problem.
<u>Tools to Have on Hand:</u> hammer (as needed), sandpaper, pipe clamps (as needed), steel tape measure (as needed)

- First, it is possible that a loose nail is blocking the passage of the drawer. In this case all you need to do is to take out the drawer and drive in the nail.
- If the drawer sags at the bottom, the simplest solution is to slide the bottom out of the drawer, turn it over, and slide the drawer back into place with the opposite side facing up. Because cabinets are made in different ways, there is no set method for sliding the bottom piece out of the drawer. It is not usually a difficult task, however. If the bottom piece is in bad repair, it is a good idea to replace it with a thin piece of plywood cut to size.

- Many wood cabinets have wood guides, with the bottom of each side serving as runners. These wood surfaces can wear down and become rutted, which makes it difficult to slide the drawer in and out. If this happens, try sanding the runners and then waxing them with paraffin wax (see drawing at right).

Drawer Falls Apart at Joints

1. A different challenge is posed when a cabinet drawer comes apart at the joints. If one or two sides remain intact, you may have to gently tap them out using a hammer and a cloth to protect the wood.

2. Once apart, clean away the old glue and any dirt that appears on the glued surface.

3. Apply wood glue to all adjoining surfaces and put the drawer back together. Attach pipe clamps across the top and bottom of the drawer while the glue is drying.

4. As soon as the clamps are in place, it is important to measure the drawer diagonally between opposite corners to make sure the drawer is square. If the measurements are not exactly equal, adjust the clamps and measure again.

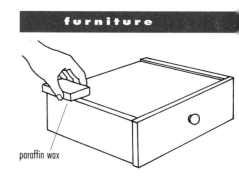

paraffin wax

To make drawers slide freely, sand the wooden runners, and then rub paraffin wax on them.

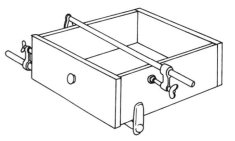

Hold newly glued drawer together with pipe clamps.

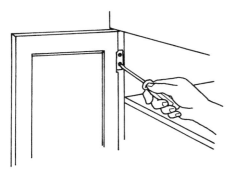

Cabinet drawers that don't stay closed may need to have their hinges tightened.

Unlatching Cabinet Door

If your cabinet door no longer latches, the problem is most likely with the hinge.

<u>Tools to Have on Hand:</u> straight-slot or Phillips screwdriver, coarse sandpaper

Begin by tightening the screws (see drawing at left). If the screw holes are enlarged, try slightly larger screws. Holes that are considerably enlarged will have to be plugged with a dowel or wooden matchsticks and glue before you insert the screws.

For doors that stick, mark the spot where the stick occurs and sand it down with coarse sandpaper. You may have to remove the door from its hinges to complete this task.

Upholstery Stains

For most spills on your upholstery, it is best to treat the problem with spot-removal techniques, rather than as a general cleaning problem. You want to avoid damaging the fabric.

With this in mind, never scrub a spot. You will only spread the stain. Soaking the spot with water or a cleaning detergent may also spread the stain. It is best to blot the stain with a clean towel. For solid spills, use a spoon to gently scrape up the spilled material, working from the edge to the center so that you don't spread the stain.

Straightening Saggy Shelves

It is not uncommon to open a closet door and find a sagging wooden shelf. These shelves sag because we overload them with too much stuff or because they are not properly supported. Fixing the problem only requires adding an additional support piece.

<u>Tools to Have on Hand:</u> straight-slot or Phillips screwdriver (as needed), pry bar (as needed), hammer, crosscut saw, stud finder (optional)

1. The first step is to remove the shelf. If the shelf is screwed in place, take a screwdriver and unfasten the screws. If the shelf is nailed in place, you will need to pry off the board. Take a pry bar and insert it between the shelf board and its support (see drawing at right). Gently pry up while being careful not to split or crack the shelf board. It is often best to pry up a little, hammer the shelf board back down, and then use the claws of your hammer to pry up the exposed nails.

2. Cut a support board about the same length as the shelf. You will want to nail or screw it into the studs along the wall. Studs are vertical pieces of wood that provide a framework for the wall. They are usually 1½ inches thick, 3½ inches deep, and are spaced every 16 inches on center along the wall (sometimes they are found to be 24 inches apart). The term "on center" means that the 16- or 24-inch measurement is taken from the center of one stud to the center of the next one. Sheetrock is nailed to the studs to form the wall. For instructions on how to locate studs, see page 126.

3. Once you find the first stud, the next one should be either 16 or 24 inches from the first one you found. Mark with a pencil the location of the studs along the path that your support piece will take.

4. Place the new support piece between the two existing support pieces and nail or screw it into place.

5. Next turn the sagging shelf piece over so that the sag is on top. Secure it to the three support pieces and that should complete the project. The sag will disappear once the shelf is loaded again.

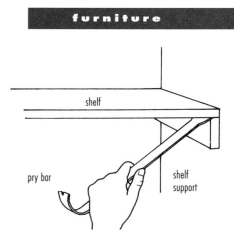

Use a pry bar to lift out the shelf.

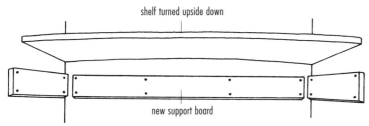

Reverse the shelf and put in place on new support board.

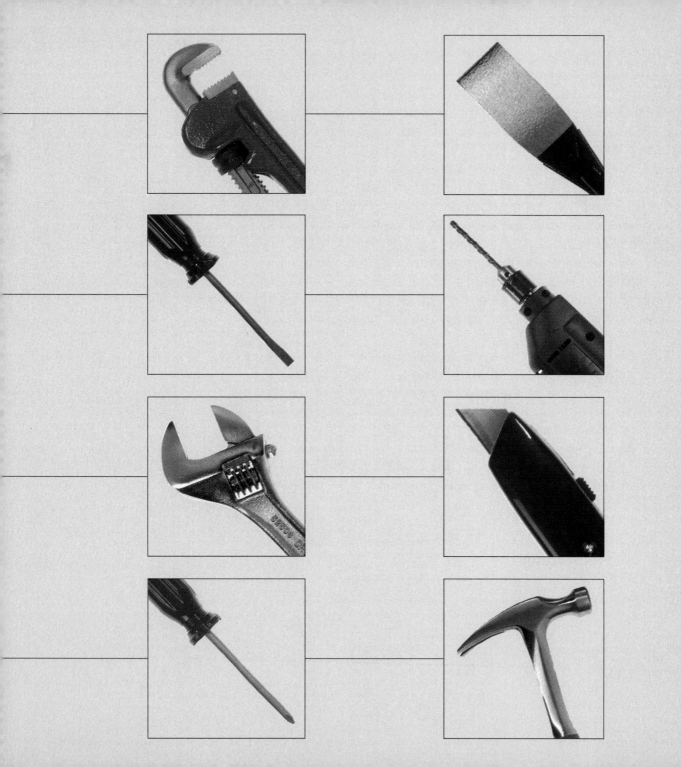

Appendices

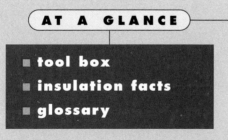

AT A GLANCE

- tool box
- insulation facts
- glossary

Stocking the Tool Box

Whether you're fixing a leaky faucet or installing a new washing machine, you need the right tools for the job. To complete your tool box, first take an inventory of what tools you already own. Begin adding new ones as projects demand and your budget allows.

When purchasing tools, start with the basics, which are described in the pages that follow. Try to strike a balance between cheap tools and those of professional quality. Inexpensive tools won't last, but you probably won't need top-of-the-line tools, either. Ask the advice of a competent salesperson at your local hardware store. This person will usually steer you in the right direction.

Tools for Measuring

Tape Measure

Because many projects require accurate measurements, your first purchase should be a **steel tape measure.** The most useful is a 25-foot tape, although a 10- to 12-foot tape will be adequate for most projects. Spend a little extra and buy one with a tape-locking device, which holds the tape in position while you make your mark.

Tape measure

Measure Twice, Cut Once

Accurate measurement is crucial for the successful completion of a project. There is nothing more frustrating or wasteful than cutting too short or too long. To make exact measurements, use a pencil with a sharp point and take the measurement twice.

Chalk Line

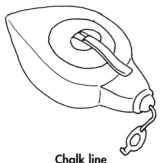

When a project requires making a long, straight line for cutting purposes, it helps to use a **chalk line.** Make sure the container has plenty of chalk before beginning. Tie the string to a nail at one end of the material to be lined or have a friend hold it. Stretch the string tight between the two points you want to line, pull the string away from the surface, and let it

Chalk line

snap. Snap the string only once or else you will have a messy line. The chalk line is also useful for wallpapering.

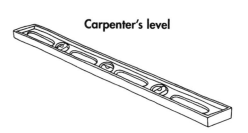

Carpenter's level

Carpenter's Level

A **carpenter's level** is useful for woodworking, masonry, wallpapering, and other projects, to make sure that a surface is level or plumb. Place the level flat on the surface and when the bubble in the window is in the middle, the object is level. A 2-foot level will be appropriate for most projects.

Electricity Testers

A different type of measuring tool is a **continuity tester,** which is used to determine whether an electrical part works. To test a part, attach the probe and clip to opposite electrical poles on the part. The continuity tester will send a current through the part and if the current passes through, the bulb on the tester will shine, indicating that the part is in good working order. If the current is blocked (meets resistance), the part is defective and the bulb will not light up.

Continuity tester

A **volt-ohm meter or voltmeter** is another device used to detect electricity. It measures the amount of voltage and resistance present, as well as tests for continuity. When the probes are touched to a circuit, the information is displayed digitally or by a dial.

A **voltage probe** also tests for voltage in receptacles and appliances. When the probe is held close to an outlet, it will light up if electricity is present.

A **neon test light** is another tool that tests for the presence of electricity in receptacles. The probes are inserted into an outlet, and if the power is on, the tester will light up

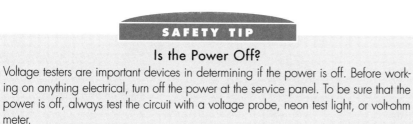

SAFETY TIP

Is the Power Off?

Voltage testers are important devices in determining if the power is off. Before working on anything electrical, turn off the power at the service panel. To be sure that the power is off, always test the circuit with a voltage probe, neon test light, or volt-ohm meter.

Tools for Fastening

Curved claw hammer

Hammers

There are many different types of hammers. The most versatile one is the **curved claw hammer,** which both drives in nails and pulls them out. It is available in various weights and with different handles. Choose the one that suits you best.

Hammer heads

Before beginning your work, check the head of the hammer to see if it is loose. Loose heads can fly off the handle and become very dangerous. A loose head with a wooden handle can often be fixed by soaking the entire hammer in water. If the handle is steel, replace it.

When using a hammer to drive a nail, start the nail with light blows, making sure to hold the handle near the end (not the head). Keep your eye on the nail, not the hammer. After the nail is able to stand on its own, remove your fingers. If you are concerned about hitting your fingers, consider using screws instead or holding the nail with a pair of long-nose pliers.

Nailing

For successful nailing, the nail should be long enough to go two-thirds of the way into the object to be fastened. Avoid nailing near the end of a board if possible, because the board may split. To reduce the chance of splitting, blunt the tip of the nail slightly. This is done by standing the nail on its head and gently tapping the tip with a hammer. When removing a nail, it often helps to slip a scrap of wood under the hammerhead to increase leverage.

Screwdrivers

A second way to fasten is with screws. Screws have some advantages over nails. They hold more firmly, they are often easier to remove, and in some cases they are easier to drive in. Screws come in two main types — the single slot screw and the Phillips screw. You will want a **straight-slot**

Phillips screwdriver

Straight-slot screwdriver

screwdriver and a **Phillips screwdriver** to be able to fasten both types of screws. Screwdrivers come in several sizes. It is probably best to purchase a large and a small screwdriver for each screw type.

It is important to use a screwdriver that fits tightly into the screw slot. If the tip of the screwdriver is too narrow, it will damage the screw head, making the screw difficult to remove after it has been inserted. This is especially true for single-slot screws.

Driving in screws is a straightforward task, although it often requires considerable strength. The first thing to keep in mind is that the longer the screwdriver blade, the more turning power you have at your disposal. If you are having difficulty, drill a hole for the screw. The drill hole should be slightly smaller in diameter than the screw so that the screw threads have something to bite into. You can purchase a portable electric screwdriver or an electric drill with a screwdriver attachment. With either tool you can drive in the screw with ease.

Drills

A **portable electric drill** is fairly inexpensive, easy to use, and very versatile. In addition to drilling holes, with the right attachments it can be used to drive in and remove screws, and to polish, buff, or sand.

Drills are purchased in terms of chuck sizes. The chuck is located at the tip of the drill and it holds the drill bit (the cutting instrument) or a drill attachment in place. The drill comes with a key that adjusts the size of the chuck's opening. A drill with a chuck size of $\frac{1}{4}$ inch or $\frac{3}{8}$ inch is perfectly adequate for most needs. When making your purchase, choose a motor that moves in reverse so that you can use the drill to unfasten screws. You will also want to buy drill bits of various sizes for drilling different hole sizes, as well as screwdriver attachments and other accessories that seem useful. Ask the salesperson to demonstrate how the drill is operated and how to adjust the chuck.

When working with your drill, make sure to grip it with two hands so that it does not wobble. Wobbling can cause the bit to break. Drill straight rather than at an angle if possible. When drilling deep holes into wood, back up the drill from time to time to remove wood chips.

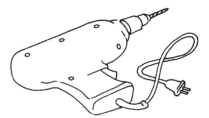

Portable electric drill

Removing Worn Screws

Removing old screws can often be a difficult task if the slot has been damaged or the screw threads stripped. Here are some tips that should help:

- Make sure the screwdriver tip fits tightly into the slot.
- You can sometimes loosen the screw by inserting the screwdriver into the head and tapping the screwdriver handle with a hammer.
- If you can twist the screw up a few turns, you can clamp a vise grip to the screw head, lock the vice grip in place, and then twist the vise grip to the left, which removes the screw.

Adhesives

Glue or other common modern adhesives do an excellent job of fastening materials together. The key to success is to pick the right adhesive for your particular project. There are many different products on the market, so it is important to read the product label carefully. You will want to determine the primary use of the product, its drying time, whether it is water resistant (moisture ruins the bonding capacity of some products), how it is applied, and whether the material is toxic to your skin or highly flammable. When applying the glue, make sure the materials to be joined are clean.

It is often recommended that a clamp or pressure device be used to hold the glued materials in place while the adhesive is drying. A **C-clamp** is the most common tool for this purpose. C-clamps come in various sizes and are inexpensive. You often need to protect the surface of your work from the clamp marks by placing a protective material between the clamp and the object. Be careful not to overtighten — finger tight is just right. You can hold together thin, light objects with clothespins.

C-clamp

Tools for Gripping

Pliers

Pliers are used to hold or grip objects. If the object is delicate (soft wood or soft metal), it is best to wrap the teeth with tape or to wrap the object in cloth so as not to scratch or mar the object you are holding.

Vise Grips

A **vise grip** is one of the most versatile tools on the market. It can be adjusted to loosen and tighten nuts and bolts much like an adjustable wrench. It has the advantage of providing a better grip on the nut or bolt, but if too much pressure is applied, it can damage the nut or bolt and make it difficult to work with in the future. It can also be used to unfasten difficult screws, as described above.

Wrenches

Most home-maintenance projects can be accomplished with either an adjustable wrench or a set of Allen wrenches. An **adjustable wrench** both loosens and tightens nuts and bolts of various sizes. However, a set of **open-end, box-end,** and **socket** wrenches will do the job easier. These wrenches have fixed jaws, and they come in different sizes — both metric and linear. They do all the things an adjustable wrench does and are especially useful for working on cars and machines, in general.

An **Allen wrench** is formed from a piece of hexagonal bar stock bent to a right angle. It comes in a set of assorted sizes. It is used to tighten or loosen set screws and screws with Allen heads, which are most often found in plumbing projects. For plumbing projects you will also need a pipe wrench. This wrench is necessary for unscrewing larger pipe connections, removing faucet stems, and for other plumbing repairs. It can also be used to unscrew large, difficult nuts.

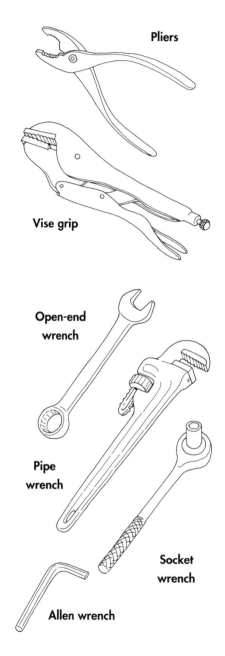

Pliers

Vise grip

Open-end wrench

Pipe wrench

Socket wrench

Allen wrench

Tools for Cutting

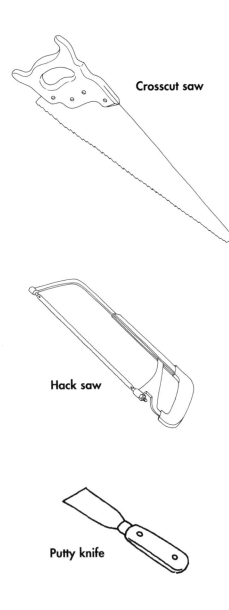

Crosscut saw

Hack saw

Putty knife

Saws

Many home projects require cutting materials to specification. Most of these projects can be completed with a crosscut saw or a hacksaw.

A **crosscut saw** is for cutting wood. It works best when it is sharp and rust free. If you have an old saw, get it sharpened before using it. The service is not expensive. You can find out where to take it by calling your local hardware store.

A good quality crosscut saw with a sharp blade can be used with relative ease. Start your cut on the side of your pencil mark that you will be discarding rather than directly on the mark so that the cut is at the correct measurement. Begin your cut by using the knuckle of your thumb to guide the saw and proceed slowly at first. As you reach the end of your cut, support the scrap end so that the wood does not splinter.

A **hacksaw** is a general purpose saw that can cut almost any material. Its primary use is cutting metal. When you purchase a hacksaw, you should also purchase a package of blades. Before purchasing the blades, check to see whether the directions on the package specify the material each blade is designed to cut. When inserting a blade into place, it is important that the teeth slant forward and that the blade fits tightly along the saw frame. The blade is tightened by the wing nut at the end of the frame.

Putty Knife

A **putty knife** is not used for cutting, but for applying putty to windows, putting spackling compound over small holes and cracks in walls, and spreading sheetrock mud.

Utility Knife

Another useful cutting tool is a **utility knife.** It comes with replaceable blades and is used to cut carpets, wallpaper, Styrofoam, and ceiling tile. When using it, make sure the blade is locked securely in place and be careful — the blade is sharp.

Utility knife

Wire Crimper

A **wire crimper** is a handy tool for doing electrical projects such as rewiring lamps, outlets, and switches, and replacing plugs. It is used for cutting and stripping wire. The wire is cut by using the tool as a pair of scissors. Place the wire inside the handle on the spot marked "wire cutters" and squeeze down. To strip wire, place the wire into one of the several holes which provides for a tight fit, twirl the crimper around the wire until the wire coating is cut, and pull off the coating. Crimping is a technique employed when you want to connect wire to a wire connector. Insert the wire into the end of the connector and squeeze down hard to seal the wire into its slot.

Wire crimper

Tin Snips

Tin snips are the tool of choice for cutting thin metal sheets. They work most effectively when the metal is up against the pivot point of the cutting blades. Because the metal tends to bend or become crimped as you approach the blade tips, stop cutting before you get there.

Standard 10-inch snips are designed for people with average grip strength. If you have trouble cutting the metal, try 12-inch snips. It is also a good idea to buy right- and left-handed snips for cutting curves. Specialty snips can be purchased for cutting intricate patterns. Ask at your local hardware store for the specific snips you will need to accomplish your project. Because metal cuts often leave sharp edges, wear gloves when doing this work.

Tin snips

Selecting Nails

The charts on these pages show a wide variety of nail styles, each designed for specific building and repair purposes. Nail sizes are designated by a "D" number. You can use the handy chart to measure your nail in order to determine its D rating. This chart is offered courtesy of Maze Nails (div. of W.H. Maze Company, Peru, IL 61354).

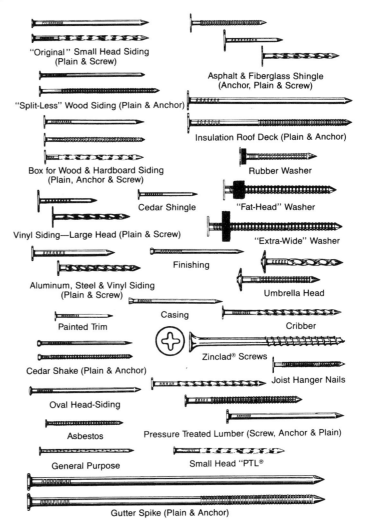

"Original" Small Head Siding (Plain & Screw)

"Split-Less" Wood Siding (Plain & Anchor)

Box for Wood & Hardboard Siding (Plain, Anchor & Screw)

Vinyl Siding—Large Head (Plain & Screw)

Aluminum, Steel & Vinyl Siding (Plain & Screw)

Painted Trim

Cedar Shake (Plain & Anchor)

Oval Head-Siding

Asbestos

General Purpose

Asphalt & Fiberglass Shingle (Anchor, Plain & Screw)

Insulation Roof Deck (Plain & Anchor)

Rubber Washer

"Fat-Head" Washer

"Extra-Wide" Washer

Cedar Shingle

Finishing

Umbrella Head

Casing

Cribber

Zinclad® Screws

Joist Hanger Nails

Pressure Treated Lumber (Screw, Anchor & Plain)

Small Head "PTL®"

Gutter Spike (Plain & Anchor)

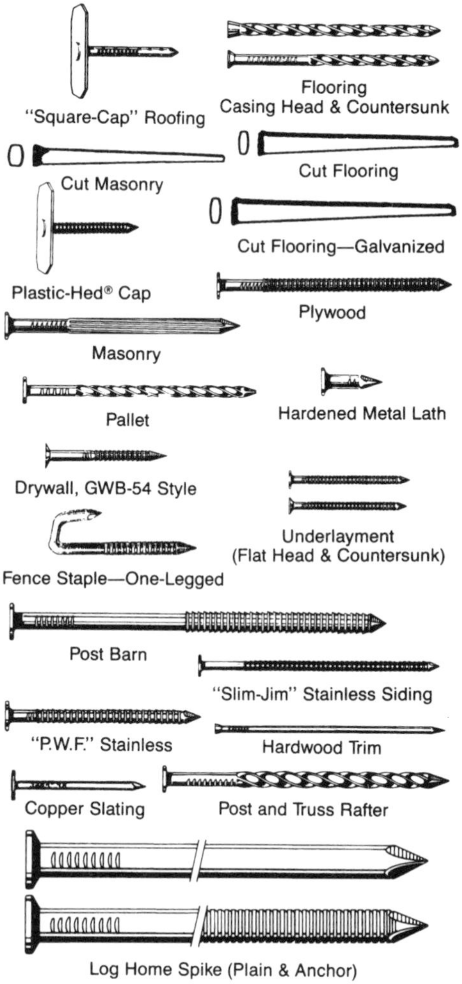

"Square-Cap" Roofing

Flooring / Casing Head & Countersunk

Cut Masonry

Cut Flooring

Plastic-Hed® Cap

Cut Flooring—Galvanized

Masonry

Plywood

Pallet

Hardened Metal Lath

Drywall, GWB-54 Style

Underlayment (Flat Head & Countersunk)

Fence Staple—One-Legged

Post Barn

"Slim-Jim" Stainless Siding

"P.W.F." Stainless

Hardwood Trim

Copper Slating

Post and Truss Rafter

Log Home Spike (Plain & Anchor)

MAZE NAILS

PENNY-INCH Nail Chart

2d	1″
3d	1¼″
4d	1½″
5d	1¾″
6d	2″
7d	2¼″
8d	2½″
9d	2¾″
10d	3″
12d	3¼″
16d	3½″
20d	4″
30d	4½″
40d	5″
50d	5½″
60d	6″
70d	7″
80d	8″
90d	9″
100d	10″

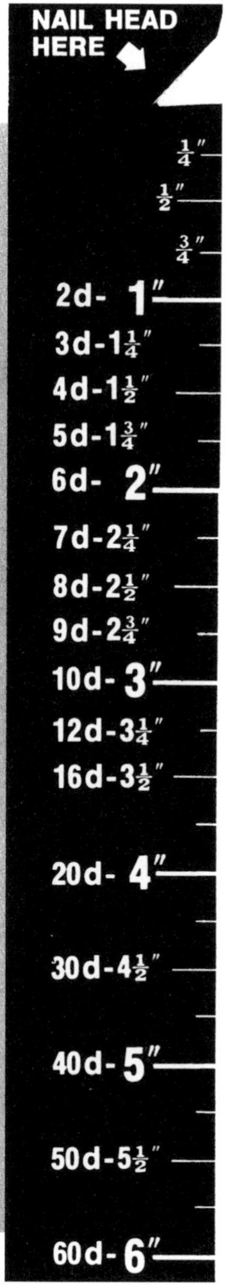

NAIL HEAD HERE

¼″
½″
¾″

2d- 1″
3d-1¼″
4d-1½″
5d-1¾″
6d- 2″
7d-2¼″
8d-2½″
9d-2¾″
10d- 3″
12d-3¼″
16d-3½″
20d- 4″
30d-4½″
40d-5″
50d-5½″
60d- 6″

Insulation Facts and Figures

The United States map below defines eight climate zones. The top chart at the right gives the ideal R-value for various areas of a home for each of the climate zones. The chart below indicates the number of inches of insulation required, depending on the type of insulating material used, for each R-value. The house diagrams on page 188 show typical sources of air leakage in a home, followed by advice on where to place insulation in order to reduce this heat loss. All of this information is courtesy of the United States Department of Energy.

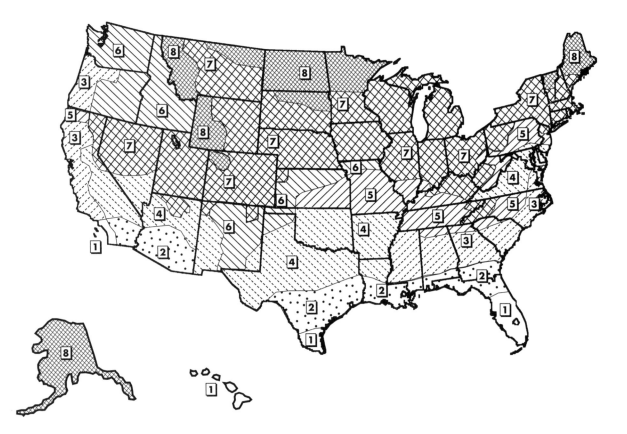

Recommended R-Values for Houses in Eight Climate Zones

ZONE	CEILINGS/ ROOFS		FLOORS OVER AN UNHEATED SPACE		EXTERIOR WOOD-FRAMED WALLS		CRAWLSPACE WALLS	
	oil, gas, heat pump	electric	oil, gas, heat pump	electric	oil, gas, heat pump	electric	oil, gas, heat pump	electric
1	19	30	0	0	0	11	11	11
2	30	30	0	0	11	11	19	19
3	30	38	0	19	11	11	19	19
4	30	38	19	19	11	11	19	19
5	38	38	19	19	11	11	19	19
6	38	38	19	19	11	11	19	19
7	38	49	19	19	11	11	19	19
8	49	49	19	19	11	11	19	19

Thicknesses for Common Insulation Material to Obtain R-Values (in inches)

R-Value	Fiberglass Batts or Blanket	Blown-in Fiberglass	Blown-in Cellulose	Blown-in Rockwool	Polystyrene Foam (EPS)	(XPS)	Polyurethane-isocyanorate Foam
R-11	3.25–3.75	4.00–5.25	3.75	3.50	2.75	2.20	1.60–1.80
R-19	5.75–6.25	7.00–8.75	6.50	6.25	4.75	3.80	2.70–3.20
R-30	9.00–9.50	11.0–14.0	10.5	9.75	7.50	6.00	4.30–5.00
R-38	11.5–12.0	14.0–17.75	13.0	12.25	9.50	7.60	5.40–6.30
R49	15.0–15.5	18.0–23.0	17.0	16.0	12.25	9.80	7.00–8.10

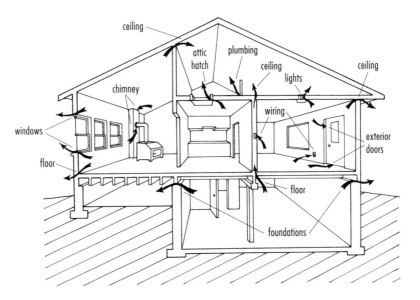

Sources of Air Leakage in the Home

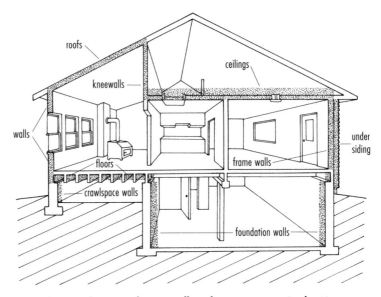

Places Where Insulation Will Reduce Heat Loss in the Home

Glossary

awning window. A single window sash hinged at the top that swings outward.

batt. A section of fiber-glass or rock-wool insulation precut to 15 or 23 inches wide by four to eight feet long.

blanket. Rolled strips of fiber-glass or rock-wool insulation that measure 15 or 23 inches wide.

carbide. A very hard material made of carbon and one or more heavy metals that is often used as a tip for drill bits.

casement window. A window hinged on the outside and opening outward with a mechanical crank used to open and close the window.

caulk. A putty-like substance used for filling cracks and sealing seams, protecting against infiltration of water or air.

ceiling joist. See *joist.*

church key. A tool with a triangular pointed head at one end for piercing cans and a rounded head at the bottom for opening bottles.

circuit. The complete path of an electric current, usually including the source of electricity.

circuit breaker. A protective switch that automatically opens, thus breaking the flow of electric current, in the event of a short or overload. See also *fuse, short circuit.*

countersink. To sink a nail or screw below the surface.

damper. On a chimney, a valve installed inside an air duct to regulate the flow of air.

diverter. The valve that switches the flow of water between two outlets of the same water source, such as the tub spigot and the showerhead.

double-hung window. A window with an upper and lower sash that slide vertically. If the upper sash is secured, the window is known as a single-hung window.

drain trap. A U-shaped drain pipe found below sinks that traps water at its bottom, forming a water seal to prevent gases, pests, and other unpleasant contaminants from entering your home.

drywall. See *sheetrock.*

fiberglass. Glass in fibrous form used for making various products, including insulation.

filament. A thin tungsten wire found in incandescent light bulbs through which electricity flows, causing it to glow, thus generating heat and light.

flue. A pipe or other air channel that carries off smoke, flame, and combustion gases to the outside air.

fluorescent light. A tubular lamp that emits light when an electric discharge excites an interior coating of fluorescent material.

fuse. An electrical safety device designed to burn out or melt if a circuit shorts or overloads, thus interrupting the electric current. See also *circuit breaker, short circuit.*

gasket. An elastic strip that forms a seal between two parts.

glazier's points. Small triangular pieces of thin metal used to hold glass in place prior to puttying.

gloss paint. Paint containing a high percentage of resin that, when dry, has a highly reflective finish.

ground fault circuit interruptor (GFCI). An electrical safety device that can sense tiny leakages of electric current at outlet sites, and will immediately cut off the flow of electricity before any harm is done.

grout. Thin mortar used to fill joints between tiles or other masonry.

hood. Over a cooking range, an enclosure or canopy provided with an inward-moving draft designed to carry off disagreeable or noxious odors, gases, or smoke.

incandescent light. A lamp in which metal filament glows when charged with electricity, emitting heat and light.

jamb. The top and sides of a door or window.

joists. Parallel horizontal framing timbers that support a floor and/or ceiling.

latex paint. A water-based paint.

lath. Strips of wood, metal, or gypsum boards that serve as a base for plaster, tiling, or stucco.

main shut-off valve. A valve found near the water meter or close to the wall where the *main water line* enters the house that controls the flow of water into the house.

main water line. Also known as the water main; the source from which all water entering the house flows, originating from a well or city water system.

mortise cut. A hole, groove, or other recess into which another element fits or passes.

on center (OC). The distance from the center of one regularly spaced framing member, such as a stud, to the next.

O-ring. A ring, usually of synthetic rubber, used as a *gasket*.

pilot hole. A small-diameter hole used to guide a nail or screw.

pilot light. A small, continuous flame used to ignite gas or oil burners when needed.

plumb. Exactly vertical (perpendicular) to the floor.

plumb line. A length of string that is weighted at one end.

polyurethane. A clear, durable, water-resistant finish used for coating stained wood to protect it against wear and tear.

primer. A first coating of paint formulated to seal raw surfaces and hold succeeding coats.

R-value. A measure of the resistance an insulating material offers to heat transfer; the higher the number, the more effective the material is at providing insulation.

sash. The frame holding the panes of glass in a window or door.

sheetrock. Also known as drywall; a plaster panel with a heavy cardboard backing that forms the main panels of a wall.

shim. A thin wedge of material used to fill in a space to make a loose fit snug or adjust the level of a surface.

short-circuit. A situation that occurs when bare electrical wires come in contact with each other or other metal parts in the circuit. *Fuses* and *circuit breakers* protect against fire that could result from the excess heat generated by a short.

spackling compound. A paste used to fill cracks in a wall or other surfaces before painting.

steam cleaner. A device used for cleaning carpets that forces a solution of cleaning detergent and hot water into the carpet and then vacuums up the dirt and water.

strike plate. The plate attached to the doorframe that engages a latch or dead bolt.

studs. Vertical pieces of wood spaced at regular intervals that provide a framework for a wall.

subfloor. The first floor, which may also serve as the finished floor, that is laid directly over the floor joists.

swag light. A simple lighting fixture consisting of an electric cord with a plug on one end and a socket and shade on the other end.

tack strips. Narrow wooden slats with tacks sticking up from them.

three-way switch. A switch, most often used for lights, that controls an electric circuit from two different switch locations.

toggle bolt. A bolt that has a nut with wings which close as the bolt is passed through a small hole. The wings spring open on the other side to keep the bolt from slipping back through the hole.

trap. See *drain trap.*

water main. See *main water line.*

weather strip. A thin material placed between a door or a window and its jambs to prevent air leakage.

wire nuts. A twist-on device used to join the ends of wires.

Index

Pilot lights
  clothes dryers, 68–69, *68*
  furnaces, 91, *92*
  ranges, 78–79, *78, 79*
  water heaters, 13, *13*
Pipes. *See* Vent pipes; Water
  supply pipes
Pipe tapper, 74, *75*
Pipe wrench, 181, *181*
Planing
  doors, 118, 119, *119*
  window sashes, 112
Pliers, 181, *181*
Plugs
  replacing, 53, *53*
  troubleshooting, **50**
Plumber's snake, 29, *29,* 31,
  31
Plumbing systems. *See also*
  Water; Water supply
  pipes; *specific fixtures*
  described, 8–9, *9*
  fix-it rules, 4, 5
  leaks, 22, 34
  turning water off, 4, 8–9
  water pressure, 22–23, **22**
  winterizing, 37

Plumb line, 139
Plungers
  unclogging sinks, 28, 30
  unclogging toilets, 32
Polyurethane, 160, 169
Power, turning off, 4, 42, 43,
  47, 145. *See also* Electrical
  systems
Power outages, 42–43, **42**
Propane, 13, 69, 78, 79
Protective gear, 102, 127, 139
Pry bar, 173, *173*
Putty knife, 182, *182*

R

Ranges. *See* Electric ranges;
  Gas ranges
Receipts, keeping, 4
Refrigerators. *See also*
  Icemakers
  condenser coils, 71, *71*
  defrost mechanism, 72
  door gasket, 72, *72*
  energy efficiency, 70, 73
  light bulbs, 73
  maintenance, 70
  smelly, 73

temperature, 70
  troubleshooting, **70**
R-value, defined, 102

S

Sanders. *See* Drum sanders
Sanding
  doors, 119
  wood floors, 160–61
Saws
  crosscut, 182, *182*
  hacksaw, 182, *182*
  wet, 155, 156
Screens
  patching, 115, *115*
  replacing, 114–15, *114,
  115*
Screwdrivers, *10,* 178–79,
  178
Screws
  loosening and tightening, 5
  removing, 180
  types and tools for, *10*
Seat grinding tool, 19, *19*
Seat wrench, 19, *19*
Self-confidence, 2
Service manuals, 4
Shelves, saggy, 172–73, *173*

Other Storey Titles You Will Enjoy

Landscaping Makes Cents: A Homeowner's Guide to Adding Value and Beauty to Your Property, by Frederick C. Campbell and Richard L. Dubé. A practical and clear guide to creating a landscape plan, determining a budget, choosing a contractor, and achieving substantial financial return on a limited budget. Includes numerous tips for the beginning landscaper and handy checklists and charts to ensure the successful completion of any project. 176 pages. Paperback. ISBN 0-88266-948-6.

Be Your Own House Contractor, by Carl Heldmann. Learn trade secrets on buying land, making estimates, getting loans, picking subcontractors, and buying materials and supplies, including smart ways to stay within budget. 144 pages. Paperback. ISBN 0-88266-266-X.

Be Your Own Home Decorator: Creating the look you love without spending a fortune, by Pauline Guntlow. Step-by-step instructions for customizing kitchens, baths, bedrooms, and living rooms. Provides unique possibilities for creating an environment that reflects personal style, regardless of cost constraints or ability. 144 pages, with full-color photographs. Paperback. ISBN 0-88266-945-1.

Small House Designs, by Kenneth R. Tremblay, Jr. & Lawrence Von Bamford, editors. A collection of award-winning, architect-designed plans for houses of 1,250 square feet or less. Judges' comments and designer's concept comments accompany plans for each project. 192 pages, with floor plans and site/elevation renderings. Paperback. ISBN 0-88266-966-4.

Play Equipment for Kids: Great Projects You Can Build, by Mike Lawrence. More than 30 easy-to-build projects for home, patio, and yard. Includes plans and photos, plus exploded how-to drawings, for attractive, durable swings, see-saws, climbing frames, playhouses, sandpits, and more. 96 pages, including color photos. Paperback. ISBN 0-88266-916-8.

These and other Storey books are available at your bookstore, farm store, garden center, or directly from Storey Books, 210 MASS MoCA Way, North Adams, MA 01247, or by calling 1–800–441–5700. Or visit our Web site at www.storey.com.